Curriculum and Assessment Policy

20 Questions for Board Members

Henry M. Brickell
Regina H. Paul

ScarecrowEducation
Lanham, Maryland • Toronto • Oxford
2005

Published in the United States of America
by ScarecrowEducation
An imprint of The Rowman & Littlefield Publishing Group, Inc.
4501 Forbes Boulevard, Suite 200, Lanham, Maryland 20706
www.scarecroweducation.com

PO Box 317
Oxford
OX2 9RU, UK

British Library Cataloguing in Publication Information Available

Library of Congress Cataloging-in-Publication Data

Brickell, Henry M.
  Curriculum and assessment policy : 20 questions for board members /
Henry M. Brickell, Regina Paul.
    p. cm.

  ISBN: 978-1-57886-209-2

  1. Curriculum planning—United States. 2. Educational tests and
measurements—United States—Planning. 3. School boards—United States—
Decision making. I. Paul, Regina H. II. Title.

LB2806.B7315 2005
379.1'58—dc22   2004065325

Contents

Acknowledgments

What we know about school boards we have learned from board members themselves. The ideas in this book are a combination of theirs and ours, with theirs being probably the more practical. The important thing is that they come from the trenches—from real school boards and real administrators and real teachers working with real kids.

Here are some of the school districts we must thank for their patience in working with us to improve the education of their students:

Bemidji Public Schools (Bemidji, Minnesota)

Binghamton City School District (Binghamton, New York)

Blue Valley Schools (Overland Park, Kansas)

Cleveland Public Schools (Cleveland, Ohio)

Columbus Public Schools (Columbus, Ohio)

Cooper Independent School District (Cooper, Texas)

Geyserville Unified School District (Geyserville, California)

Greenwich Public Schools (Greenwich, Connecticut)

Grosse Pointe Public Schools (Grosse Pointe, Michigan)

Norwalk Public Schools (Norwalk, Connecticut)

Plainedge Public School District (Massapequa, New York)

Richmond Public Schools (Richmond, Virginia)

Savannah-Chatham County Public Schools (Savannah, Georgia)

School District of Brown Deer (Brown Deer, Wisconsin)

Township High School District 211 (Palatine, Illinois)

Unified School District 261 (Haysville, Kansas)

Valley View Public Schools (Valley View, Illinois)

Special thanks goes to the Texas Association of School Boards, which has invited us to talk about curriculum and assessment with hundreds of board members over the past decade.

A Job for Civilians

This introductory chapter is taken from the authors' book Time for Curriculum, *published by the National Schools Boards Association in 1988.*

The most remarkable thing about our remarkable country is this: Ordinary citizens control almost every major public institution. No matter how many expert professionals are on the payroll, they do not have the last word. Somewhere above them, above the top of the pyramid of experts, is a group of civilians. They have the last word. They are not as expert as the experts, but they have the last word. They may know less about the operations than anyone on the payroll. Still, they have the last word.

Does this make sense? What it makes is democracy. Government of the people, by the people, for the people. We, the people, govern ourselves. The professional experts do not govern us. We govern them; they serve us.

That is a particularly American idea. It may be the most American idea of all. No nation uses it more. It is our favorite form of governance. We use it for villages, townships, cities, counties, states, regions, the nation. We use it for sewers, police, roads, firefighting, rivers, libraries, prisons, forests, the military—every government function, without exception; all staffed by experts, without exception; and all governed by civilians.

Every government worker can say:

"The people who run this place know less about it than I do."

And we can say:

"That's right. The mayor knows less about police work than a detective does, and the city council knows even less. The governor knows less about the state universities than the professors do, and the legislature knows even less. The president knows less about the Air Force than the colonels do, and the Congress knows even less. Good thing.

"We wouldn't want your agency run by people who know as much about it as you do. We want it run by people who know less about it. Your problem is that you know too much. You are an expert, an insider. If you were in charge, you might run the place for the benefit of the insiders. We want the place run by outsiders. We want government of the outsiders, by the outsiders, for the benefit of the outsiders. We do not want government of the insiders, by the insiders, for the benefit of the insiders. That would be un-American. If you don't like that idea, you might try another country. You can leave here and travel in any direction, except north, and find plenty of them."

Government of the insiders, by the insiders, for the benefit of the insiders is extremely popular today, just as it has been throughout history. From the beginning of time, it has been almost every society's idea of how to govern. It's just not ours.

Insiders make bad governors because they focus on the operations; outsiders make good governors because they focus on the results. Insiders prefer certain operations. Because they know so much about operations, they develop strong opinions about *how* things should be done. Outsiders do not know enough to prefer certain operations. They may not even care about the operations. The consequence is that insiders on the board tend to judge the institution by its operations; outsiders on the board tend to judge the institution by its results.

The preference of insiders for certain operations may result in pervasive bad effects if they become board members:

- They pull operational matters up onto the board agenda, where they don't belong.

- They argue eyeball to eyeball with the chief executive about operations: one expert versus another expert.

- They press the chief executive between board meetings to adopt certain operations they favor.

- They are excessively sympathetic toward employees—their wants, their opinions, their grievances—and too subject to pressure from employees.

We don't want insiders on the governing board, much as they might want to be there. Nobody understands this better than the top executive who works for the board. Ask any minister, hospital administrator, or museum director, "Who makes the worst board members?" They will tell you, "Another minister, another hospital administrator, another museum director."

Good chief executives want to be judged by their results. This gives them a weak allegiance to current operations. They are willing to change their operations in any way necessary to get good results. In this respect, they think like good board members, an essential job skill for any chief executive: Talk like an expert, think like a board member.

Perhaps you are wondering whether any of this applies to the public schools. All of it does. The point is this: *Because* you are a civilian rather than an expert in education, you are qualified to govern the public schools.

Curriculum and Assessment Are Too Complex for Civilians —Or Are They?

Curriculum and assessment are not as complex for a civilian member of a school board as medicine is for a civilian member of a hospital board.

But curriculum and assessment are more complex than school transportation, more than school insurance, more than school building maintenance, and more than school tax rates.

Curriculum and assessment are so complex that school board members tend to leave them to the educators, just as hospital board members tend to leave medicine to the doctors. That is too bad, because curriculum and assessment are not only more complex, but also more important than transportation, insurance, maintenance, and tax rates. It might be all right for school board members to leave those other matters to the educators, but not curriculum and assessment. School board members should control those.

This book is designed to help you adopt good policies for doing just that.

Overview of the Policy Clock

The six key decision points in the operations of a school district can be laid out around the face of a clock, making them both simple to understand and easy to communicate. There are documents at each of the six points:

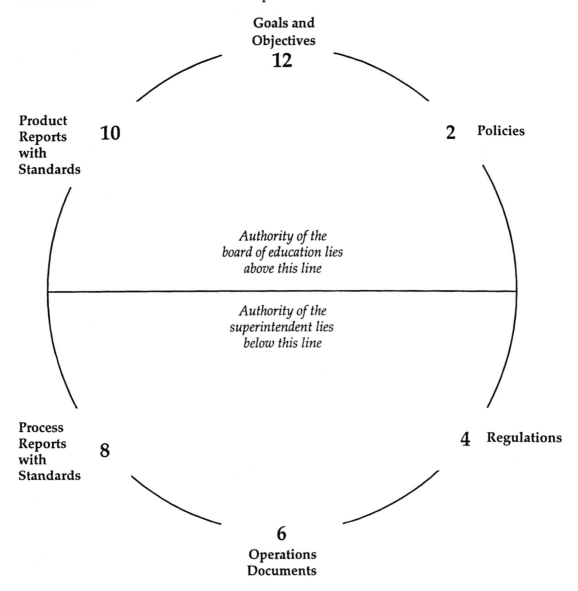

Clockwise, the goals and objectives guide the choice of policies that will shape the schooling required to produce the learning called for by the goals and objectives. Those policies frame the regulations that will further shape the schooling. That schooling will be described first in operations documents and then in process reports. The results of that schooling will be described later in product reports, with those results compared to the goals and objectives, thus closing the circle.

Counterclockwise, unsatisfactory product reports require a look first at process reports and then at operations documents to find flaws that require corrections in the schooling by modifying regulations and/or policies to increase the likelihood of accomplishing the goals and objectives.

12 o'clock—*Goals and Objectives*

These are descriptions of what students must learn in school—what they must know, feel, and do. Curriculum goals and objectives are the *ends* of schooling. They are prepared and proposed by the superintendent and the professional staff and then judged and adopted by the board. Until they are set, the clock cannot start ticking.

2 o'clock—*Policies*

These are *general means* statements, prepared and proposed by the superintendent and other school personnel and then judged and adopted by the board to guide the superintendent and other school personnel in achieving the curriculum goals and objectives that the board adopted at 12 o'clock. Policies are *guides for discretionary action.* They must truly guide the superintendent and other school personnel in what to do; and, yet, they must allow discretion in making fine-grained decisions about the detailed means for achieving the 12 o'clock goals and objectives.

4 o'clock—*Regulations*

These are *detailed means* statements for achieving the 12 o'clock curriculum goals and objectives. Regulations are *specifications of required action*, directing school personnel as to what they must do. They are prepared and adopted by the superintendent (usually upon the recommendation of other school personnel) to carry out the policies adopted by the board. Regulations are not adopted by the board.

6 o'clock—*Operations Documents*

These are the detailed plans, procedures, schedules, announcements, and memoranda used daily to operate the schools, pursuant to the policies and regulations. They are designed and written by the superintendent, other central office administrators, building administrators, professional committees, and individual teachers as they exercise their authority. Operations documents control a thousand details in the operations of instruction, buildings and grounds, finance, personnel, student activities, and community relations.

8 o'clock—*Process Reports with Standards*

These are reports designed by the superintendent and other school personnel that tell whether the policies and regulations are being followed and whether the operations are being carried out to standards set by the superintendent. They tell whether the planned processes are in place. Prepared by the superintendent and other administrators to monitor their own activities, process reports can provide distant early warnings of possible failure to reach the 12 o'clock curriculum goals and objectives—warnings that come early enough to trigger corrective action.

10 o'clock—*Product Reports with Standards*

These are reports that tell the superintendent and the board the degree to which the 12 o'clock curriculum goals and objectives have been achieved. Thus, they are reports of student learning—knowledge, attitudes, and skills —compared to standards recommended by the superintendent and adopted by the board to judge student learning. Product reports tell the board whether the order it placed at 12 o'clock was filled by the superintendent, staff, and students.

12 O'Clock—Goals and Objectives

There are no goals and objectives for school districts except what students learn—the *ends* of schooling. Everything else, without exception, is a *means* to those ends.

Thus, it is not a goal to sell a bond issue, not an objective to purchase and install new computers, not a goal to hold staff development workshops, not an objective to fill all teacher vacancies by July. Those are all, without exception, means for achieving the real goals and objectives.

Curriculum goals and objectives are the real ones. They are the *what* of learning, not the *how* of teaching. The how of teaching may be described later at 2 o'clock and 4 o'clock and even 6 o'clock. But the curriculum goals and objectives go first—at 12 o'clock. They start the clock ticking.

If the descriptions of student learning—that is, the curriculum goals and objectives—are to guide the daily choice of means at 2 and 4 and 6, those descriptions must be clear and vivid. Further, they must be shared and understood by all of those responsible for student learning: teachers, administrators, parents, and students themselves.

A Pyramid of Possibilities

Curriculum goals and objectives for student learning can be stated at different levels of specificity. There are merits and demerits in using each level. For example, the less specific the statements, the fewer it takes to describe an educated student—an attractive economy in words. On the other hand, the more specific the statements, the more likely they can be accurately judged or even measured—an attractive form of proof.

The term *goal* is customarily used in the profession to mean a description more general than the term *objective*, indeed to mean something that summarizes a set of objectives and that results from achieving a set of objectives. Even so, curriculum goals themselves can be written at various levels of specificity and so can curriculum objectives.

Imagine an infinite intellectual pyramid of possible curriculum goals and objectives, ranging from "reaches her potential" at the apex to "names the capitals of the 50 states" at the base. Moving up the pyramid, one finds increasingly broad statements with wider and wider "coverage." Moving down the pyramid, one finds increasingly detailed statements that are more interpretable and easier to evaluate. Educators over the years have created or assembled countless collections of curriculum goals and objectives describing desirable student learning in various grades and various subjects at every imaginable level of specificity.

A school district must choose the level or levels at which it wants to describe student learning. For classroom teachers, statements have to be quite specific for planning lessons and units, selecting materials, and evaluating learning. The same is true for principals making classroom visits and for evaluators designing tests. All of them need quite specific curriculum objectives. For the superintendent, on the other hand, curriculum statements may need to be broader for communicating to the public what is most and least important for students to learn. The same is true for other central administrators who are concerned with broader issues, such as whether reading is more important than writing, whether mathematics is more important than science, whether all students are to learn the performing arts or only students with special talent. All of them need somewhat broader curriculum goals.

Priorities can be set at the top of the pyramid with broad goals, but teaching and evaluation must take place at the bottom with specific objectives.

Most school districts find that two levels are sufficient for describing desired student learning: one level for curriculum goals and one level for curriculum objectives. Defining more than two levels is a difficult intellectual exercise, and maintaining a system with more than two levels is even more difficult. More important, two levels are enough to satisfy all users for all uses: enough to guide the operations, enough to evaluate the results.

Here are some good examples of the two levels:

Sample Curriculum Goals

- Writes in a clear and organized fashion
- Estimates answers to mathematical problems with reasonable accuracy
- Analyzes current U.S. social, political, and economic problems
- Believes in conserving natural resources
- Speaks a second language
- Uses computer software to create and manipulate databases and spreadsheets
- Displays good sportsmanship when playing with others
- Chooses a place for the arts in his or her life

Sample Curriculum Objectives

- Develops multi-paragraph compositions using stated comparisons and contrasts
- Finds the perimeter of a square, given the length of only one side
- Summarizes the story of the Boston Tea Party of 1773
- Builds series and parallel circuits
- Uses the definite articles *la* and *le*
- Uses the basic formatting commands in a word processing program
- Uses warm-up and cool-down activities routinely when exercising
- Sings two-part rounds

Curriculum goals and objectives should be challenging, comprehensive, clearly written, and free of educational jargon. They should be understandable to all of a school district's stakeholders, including parents and, of course, the board.

Once proposed by the superintendent and adopted by the board, the curriculum goals and objectives become the teaching and learning targets of all school personnel as well as of parents and of students themselves.

Remember that curriculum goals and objectives are the ends of schooling; all else is just the means.

2 O'Clock—Policies

A policy is a *guide for discretionary action* adopted by the board of education to guide the operations of the school district. A policy is narrow enough to give clear guidance as to what kinds of action the board considers appropriate, yet broad enough to leave room for discretion in deciding exactly what actions to take.

Policy making should be a way of life for a board. It should be continuous—not the subject of a special project each decade or even of an annual review. The Board should not turn away from its regular work to make policy. Making policy should be the board's regular work. Discussing, debating, and adopting policies should occur at each board meeting. That is what it means to govern the school operations.

From the board's perspective, policies give it maximum control—more control than it can get by making regulations (that is, *specifications of required action*), more than it can get by making case-by-case decisions, more than it can get by reviewing the superintendent's detailed decisions. This is because a policy has breadth. It covers many different circumstances and countless cases. It even reaches out ahead and controls circumstances and cases not yet considered when the board adopted it.

Moreover, a policy is always there, even when the board is not. Seven days a week, 12 months a year, it speaks for the board.

Rather than deciding a specific case, the board should debate and adopt a policy covering cases like that. A policy discussion lifts the topic above the emotion surrounding the case and lets the board take a less pressured action. Once the board makes the policy, the superintendent can decide the case.

From the superintendent's perspective, policies give him or her maximum freedom to administer school operations—more than following a precedent, more than checking with the board president, more than waiting for a board meeting to ask. This is because a policy speaks for the entire board—or at least for the majority. And it speaks from a time when the board was deliberating not a single case, but a general line of action, based on one or more principles. That is what makes it stable and predictive of the board's future preferences.

There is more:

1. Policies summarize the accumulated wisdom of previous boards as well as previous superintendents. And they do it in the best possible form for easy use by the current board and superintendent.

2. Policies save an enormous amount of time for the board because they make whole classes of decisions in a single stroke, instruct the superintendent on how to decide cases without elaborate discussion in board meetings, and delegate a thousand decisions that never need to come to the board.

3. Policies are the best possible "workshop in print" for newly elected board members, drawing a clear boundary between the authority of the board and the authority of the superintendent—a boundary that may be awkward for the superintendent to draw.

Policies are the way for the board to guide and simultaneously to free the superintendent in every aspect of school operations:

- Community relations
- Administration
- Business and noninstructional operations
- Personnel
- Students
- Instruction

The board's policy manual should have a table of contents that breaks down each of these six broad areas so that the hundreds of topics that must be addressed in running school operations can be classified into one of the six categories and, as it becomes necessary, made the subject of a policy.

A policy can be expressed in a phrase, a sentence, a paragraph, a page, or a policy paper. Here are some examples of very short policies from outside the domain of education:

- Safety first
- Do unto others as you would have them do unto you.
- All the news that's fit to print
- Look before you leap.
- Speak softly and carry a big stick.

All of them give firm guidance; none of them dictate specific action. Those are the twin tests of a good policy statement. Many, many boards adopt "policies" that fail one of these tests. Most frequently, policies fail on the first test—that is, they are so general that they give no guidance at all. They are little more than philosophy and platitudes. Such policies are not worth having. They will not help the superintendent make good decisions, and they will not help the board wield its authority wisely.

Here are some brief policy statements on education matters:

- All elementary school classrooms shall be racially balanced.

- The RTA shall be used to transport secondary school students to and from school when the total travel time, including walking, is reasonable.

- Periodic evaluations by the community of both the attractiveness and the effectiveness of the print media published by the school district shall be made and reported to the board of education.

- First priority in the use of school time in the elementary grades shall be given to teaching mathematics. A substantial amount of instructional time each day shall be scheduled for teaching mathematics to elementary school students.

- Repeated attempts shall be made to contact parents about student absences whenever they are not reached by the initial attempt.

Once made, a policy can be executed or administered by the superintendent in one of two ways: (1) by making a single decision about a single case in keeping with the policy; or (2) by adopting regulations in keeping with the policy—that is, regulations that will control many single decisions made by others in the future. Both methods are necessary, but making regulations is an especially efficient way for the superintendent to exercise his or her discretion by making one decision that controls many others. We turn the clock hands to 4 o'clock to see how regulations work.

4 O'Clock—Regulations

A regulation is a *specification of required action* adopted by the superintendent or other administrators to guide the operations of the school district. A regulation tells exactly what must be done, often tells by whom it must be done, and sometimes tells when and how and where they must do it. It deliberately leaves little or no room for judgment.

Making regulations is one major method used by administrators to carry out the board's intentions as expressed in board policies. Administrators make regulations when they want to leave little or no room for deviation—when they want to be positive that certain things will be done by certain people at certain times in certain ways.

Boards should not make regulations for two reasons, both extremely important:

1. Board members cannot know enough about the daily details of school operations to debate or decide upon good regulations.
2. Exceptions to regulations need to be made in special situations—sometimes immediately—and the board cannot be there to make those exceptions. Any exceptions to regulations must, of course, be made inside the boundary of board policy.

Nevertheless, the board can exert strong influence on regulations by the way it shapes its policies. This is because administrative regulations must conform to those policies.

There are a few topics on which the superintendent and other administrators do not actually want the power to make exceptions. They want to say to teachers or parents or students or taxpayers: "The Board of Education requires this. There is nothing I can do." On such topics, the board itself can adopt a regulation proposed by the superintendent, effectively tying administrative hands by pre-deciding against every specific request for an administrative exception.

Because only those who make the rules can break the rules, whoever makes a regulation must expect requests for exceptions. Whenever the board adopts a regulation, it automatically draws those requests onto its own agenda. Since dealing with such requests is seldom a good use of the board's time, the board should adopt regulations only on those few topics on which the superintendent and other administrators do not want the traffic or cannot handle the pressure of making exceptions. Those topics might include these, for example:

- Age of entrance to kindergarten
- Travel expense allowances for board members
- Requirements for making up school days lost because of weather
- Student dress codes
- The formula used for selecting the graduating class's valedictorian

Regulations are useful as evidence in litigation—more useful than policies because regulations are specific. The courts expect government agencies—including the public schools—to be systematic, to publish clear rules, to give fair notice, and to act without bias. Regulations constitute written proof (assuming that they are administered as written) that the school government meets the Constitutional tests applied by the courts in deciding cases.

Many regulations are negotiated into union contracts. Indeed, those contracts tend to be collections of personnel regulations agreed to by the board and the union, deliberately taking the power to make exceptions out of the hands of administrators. The strongest single argument advanced by unions in the past in favor of labor contracts has been the need to prevent arbitrary, unfair, and biased actions by administrators. Even today, a common cause for grievances is alleged attempts by administrators to make exceptions to what the contract requires. Once a regulation is embedded in a contract, only the board and the union, acting jointly, can make changes or make exceptions.

A regulation, like a policy, can be expressed in a phrase, a sentence, a paragraph, a page, or a handbook. Here are some examples of very short regulations from outside the domain of education:

- No smoking
- Stop on red.
- This side up
- One to a customer
- Close cover before striking.
- Three strikes and you're out.

All of them dictate specific actions; none of them leaves room for judgment or permits deviation. Yet, all of them are subject to wise exceptions in special circumstances: We do not stop on red when the traffic officer waves us on through; we do turn the container on its side rather than tearing down the doorway to make the delivery; and the store owner may give two to her best customer if asked.

Here are some brief regulations on education matters, although regulations can, of course, contain far more detail than these:

- PTAs will not be charged for the use of school facilities, regardless of the time, length, or type of use.
- Police will be given the name, age, grade, address, and telephone number of any student bringing a firearm onto school property within four hours of the occurrence.
- Vendors' bills must be received in the district's business office no later than 4:30 p.m. on the fifth business day preceding the board meeting at which payment will be requested.
- Each teacher retiring after 10 or more years of service to the district will be presented with a framed letter of appreciation signed by the President of the Board of Education and the Superintendent of Schools.

In some school districts, in the name of decentralization, the board may adopt a policy intended to delegate authority directly to individual schools, purposely eliminating districtwide administrative regulations, as might be the case with a board policy like this:

> Elementary schools shall be strongly encouraged to celebrate the diversity of students in their own individual buildings by favorable recognition of such differences as the students' native languages, holidays, games, foods, and dress. Schools shall be permitted great flexibility and creativity in how they conduct such celebrations.

A Note about Bylaws: Bylaws are regulations adopted by the board to control its relations with itself. They regulate matters like meeting schedules, size of a quorum, titles of board officers, duties of officers, and related matters of board procedures. Bylaws may be filed in the back of the board's policy manual, but they are regulations, not policies.

6 O'Clock—Operations Documents

Most documents created or used by a school district do not contain goals or objectives, policies, regulations, process reports, or product reports. They are instead the countless other documents used to do the daily business of the schools.

Because they are not tools to govern or to evaluate the operations, they are of little use to the board and thus should be of little interest to the board. But they are essential to the superintendent and other administrators.

Guided both by the framework of board policies set at 2 o'clock and administrative regulations set at 4 o'clock as well as by the set of required process reports at 8 o'clock and required product reports at 10 o'clock for which they must collect information, these documents make orderly school operations possible.

While no list can do justice to the full range of operations documents, the list below suggests their diversity:

- Records of principals' classroom observations
- Student handbooks
- Bus schedules
- Administrative bulletins
- Lunch menus
- Solicitations of price quotations for goods wanted
- Bills from vendors
- Maintenance manuals
- Lists of advisory committee members
- Parental permission slips
- Blueprints
- Curriculum committee reports
- Emergency drill procedures
- Newsletters to parents
- Purchase orders
- Personnel records
- Lists of substitute teachers
- Employment applications
- Memoranda setting up interscholastic sports schedules
- Correspondence with state officials

Many school district "documents" are both created and filed in electronic form and are displayed on paper when needed. This discussion makes no distinction between the two since the format does not affect the authority or the responsibility of either the board or the superintendent regarding their content.

Some operations documents quote or paraphrase items from documents located at other points on the clock. A handbook for teachers or an application blank for prospective employees or an instruction sheet for vendors may quote from a policy or a regulation. Such 6 o'clock operations documents do not *establish* those policies or regulations; they merely cite them in convenient form.

District curriculum guides—widely used operations documents—usually draw from other points on the clock. The typical curriculum guide contains 12 o'clock curriculum objectives and sometimes curriculum goals. It may contain selected 4 o'clock regulations and occasionally 2 o'clock policies. It may contain forms to collect information for 8 o'clock process reports. It often contains test questions or other assessment techniques that provide some of the data for 10 o'clock product reports. Again, the curriculum guide does not *establish* any of these, but simply assembles them in a single location convenient for teachers. The bulk of the curriculum guide, of course, consists of suggested teaching activities and teaching materials.

One approach that some school districts use to decentralize authority from the central office to the individual schools or to clusters of schools is to establish regulations only on matters requiring districtwide uniformity. That leaves the individual schools or clusters free to conduct operations on other matters as they elect, including designing their own operations documents—as long as they stay within the boundaries of board policy.

Leaving the writing of operations documents to the administrators and other school personnel shows respect for their abilities. More importantly, the pre-service training that many of them received in colleges of education and their daily experiences in the trenches equip them well for that kind of work. That is why most operations documents used by schools turn out to be entirely adequate.

On the other hand, what usually needs work are the documents at other points on the clock, points at which the board and the superintendent can exert greater influence and can have greater impact with less effort than at 6 o'clock.

Because the board can gain sufficient control and oversight of school district operations with 12 o'clock goals and objectives, 2 o'clock policies, and 10 o'clock product reports of student learning, it can and should leave the 6 o'clock operations documents to the administrators and other school personnel.

8 O'Clock—Process Reports with Standards

Process reports are gauges as to whether—and how well—the 2 o'clock policies and the 4 o'clock regulations are being carried out. They tell nothing about the *ends* of schooling—student learning—but tell only whether the *means* of schooling actually being used match the means of schooling envisioned and indeed required by the policies and regulations. An unsatisfactory match is a distant early warning that the *actual means* may not produce the *intended ends*—that is, that the schooling being used may not achieve the student learning called for at 12 o'clock.

We might well call process reports "administrative reports" (*to* the administrators rather than from them) because the superintendent and other administrators need to know whether things are running as they should. And they need to know soon enough to correct bad operations before they cause harm. There are many possibilities for prospective harm, including damage to public relations, damage to school finances, damage to legal liability, damage to teacher morale, or, most important, damage to student learning.

Process reports are designed to describe ongoing operations in such a way that they reveal success or failure, whichever is the case. To do that, they must contain more than raw data, whether verbal or statistical. Data are meaningless in and of themselves. Data cannot reveal either success or failure unless the descriptions they provide are compared to some kind of standards for how those descriptions should look. That is, the facts must be judged or else they are not worth the money it takes to collect and report them—except perhaps to satisfy outside legal requirements. All judgments require standards.

A process standard is a template for examining whether or how an activity *is being conducted*, not for examining the *results* of that activity. It is a standard for judging how a game is being played, not for judging the final score; a standard for judging the way an automobile is being driven, not for judging whether it reaches its destination; a standard for judging a teacher's processes—enthusiasm, creativity, warmth, orderliness, clear explanations, fair testing, unbiased grading—not for judging the student learning that results.

There are two kinds of process standards, each having its advantages and disadvantages:

- *Absolute standards*—They describe desired district processes irrespective of what other districts are doing.

  Here is one standard of that type: There will be no incidents of vandalism.

- *Comparative standards*—They describe desired district processes expressed as comparisons to what other districts are doing.

  Here is one standard of that type: Costs per student mile for bus transportation will be at or below the average cost in similar districts.

Once either absolute or comparative standards have been set and data have been displayed against those standards, an analysis can be made about the success or failure of the activity. Of course, those successes and failures should be looked at over time in order to learn whether things are getting better, getting worse, or staying the same in the district.

A process report can describe any activity in the school district. Here are examples of common and uncommon topics covered by such reports:

- Revenues and expenses
- PTA meeting attendance as a percent of PTA membership
- Substitute teacher turnover rates
- Proportion of high school students electing advanced academic courses
- Frequency of parents' visits to schools
- Progress of construction projects
- Number and types of personnel grievances
- Student attendance rates
- Library book circulation as a fraction of holdings
- Competitive grants received from outside sources
- Student mobility into and out of the school district
- Number and types of student disciplinary infractions
- Proportion of contracts awarded to minority vendors
- Number of career internships held by high school students
- Incidence of communicable diseases among elementary school children
- Emergency equipment maintenance service calls
- Proportion of teachers completing graduate degrees
- Actions taken on recommendations of vocational advisory committees
- Number of and attendance at inservice workshops held for teachers

Even this brief list demonstrates that many kinds of process reports are imaginable—more than any school budget could afford. Here are some criteria for setting priorities among all those imaginable and deciding which reports are worth producing:

1. This process affects student learning.
2. This process affects the safety and security of students and staff.
3. This process affects the budget.
4. This process affects legal liabilities.
5. This process affects the public's image of the district.

Unfortunately, almost all reports appearing on board agendas are process reports (unaccompanied by standards for judgment). As we said earlier, these are "administrative reports." They effectively invite the board out of governance and into administration—that is, out from macro-guidance and into micro-management. Rather than spending its time examining product reports of student learning, comparing them to its established goals and objectives, and adjusting its policies to increase learning, the board is led to lean over the superintendent's shoulder and offer management advice and even directives about school processes.

Board members lack the expertise for this. Moreover, it is a weak way for the board to use its power. Every moment studying process reports is a moment lost from studying product reports. The board should leave process reports to the superintendent and the other administrators and insist instead on being brought product reports that can be judged against the board's standards for student learning, as explained at 10 o'clock.

10 O'Clock—Product Reports with Standards

The product of schooling is an educated person. Thus, a product report is a report of learning accomplished by the students—what kindergartners have learned about the alphabet, second graders about dribbling, fourth graders about igneous rock, seventh graders about musical notation, ninth graders about quadratic equations, eleventh graders about James Madison, twelfth graders about speaking French, or whatever the superintendent recommended and the board decided students should learn when it set its 12 o'clock curriculum goals and objectives.

The blueprint for the product reports is those curriculum goals and objectives. Every objective can be the basis for a test question—whether that "test question" is an essay, an experiment, a trombone solo, an analysis of original historical sources, a speech, a soccer match, a multiple-choice question, or some other way for students to demonstrate what they have learned. The answers to such questions become the 10 o'clock product reports placed on the board's table. The answers to the "test questions" about a cluster of related objectives become the evidence as to whether the *goal* represented by the *cluster of objectives* has been achieved. For example, evidence that the goal "writes persuasively" has been accomplished by eleventh graders is assembled from evidence that they have learned the various aspects of persuasive writing described by the cluster of objectives specifying a variety of persuasive writing skills.

Unless the board—and, of course, the superintendent, who will create and present the product reports to the board—has product reports matching its 12 o'clock curriculum goals and objectives, it cannot know any of these:

- To what degree it has succeeded or failed as a board
- Whether and how it must adjust its 2 o'clock policies to produce the student learning it seeks
- Whether the superintendent and the professional staff are performing as intended
- Whether the taxpayers are being well served

As to the timing of product reports, the board can have them as often as it wants. It need not wait until year's end. It can have them as often as the end of each marking period, or quarterly, or by semester, as it chooses. It can have the superintendent establish a rotating schedule of reports grade by grade and subject by subject—for example, high school mathematics and music at the end of the first quarter, middle school art and social studies at the end of the second, elementary school language arts and physical education at the end of the third, and so on throughout the school and calendar year.

Of course, having frequent product reports can get expensive. Exactly as with process reports, a board might dream of having more than any school budget could afford. Here are some criteria for a responsible board to use in setting priorities among possible product reports:

1. This report provides evidence about student learning in the most important school subjects.
2. This report provides evidence about student learning at key transition grades—from elementary to middle school, from middle to high school, and from high school to college.

3. This report provides evidence about student learning in the grades and subjects in which the district has performed worst in recent years.

The superintendent and the professional staff will, of course, have to design and administer a testing program to generate the reports the board wants. That program could include commercially available nationally standardized tests, state tests (where available and/or required), and locally made tests matched perfectly to the board's 12 o'clock curriculum goals and objectives. Of course, the guidance for such a testing program would come to the superintendent and the professional staff from the board itself when it adopts its 2 o'clock policy on testing.

Exactly as with process reports, the information in product reports—whether expressed in words, numbers, or graphics; whether recorded on paper, tape, or disk; whether visual or auditory or both—is meaningless unless accompanied by standards for judgment. Any individual may have a standard for judging student learning—any teacher, any parent, any administrator, any board member. That is not enough. The board as the legally constituted governing body must have standards for judging student learning—that is, collective standards agreed to by a majority.

And exactly as with process reports, each type of standard has pros and cons:

- *Absolute standards*—They describe desired district results regardless of what other districts are producing.

  Here is one standard of that type: 80 percent of the fifth graders will pass the district's own science test with a score of 70 percent correct or better.

- *Comparative standards*—They describe desired district results expressed as comparisons to what other districts are producing.

  Here is one standard of that type: Average district test scores in reading in each of the elementary grades will be at or above the 85th national percentile.

And exactly as with process reports, once either absolute or comparative standards have been set and data have been displayed against those standards, an analysis can be made about whether the district achieved the desired results. Further, those achievements should be looked at over time in order to determine whether learning is improving in the district. In fact, the board may want to set progressively higher standards for the next three to five years as a way of calling for continuous improvement.

The most powerful way for a board to exert its authority over the schools is not to hire a new superintendent, not to perform well at televised board meetings, not to sell a bond issue and preside over the construction of a new school—important as those are. The most powerful way is for the board to keep its eyes trained on product reports, to judge the evidence of student learning against its standards, and to discuss those judgments with the superintendent—especially when the results are not satisfactory. Producing learning is, to repeat, the only reason for the schools to exist, the only reason for the board to exist.

How To Use the Discussion Guides

The two most important points on the face of the clock for you to control are the 12 o'clock curriculum goals and objectives and the 10 o'clock product reports with standards. To put it another way, the two most important things for you to decide are what you want students to learn and what you will take as proof that they are learning it.

Because the board exerts its control by adopting policies (*guides for discretionary action*) at 2 o'clock, it follows that the most important policies the board can adopt are those that it uses to control 12 o'clock and 10 o'clock. Making those policies requires the board to debate its way through a thicket of complex issues, many of which turn out to be related such that a decision on one issue affects the board's decisions on others.

This is a trip that some of you board members may not have made before. So you will need your superintendent as your guide.

The remainder of this book is a set of discussion guides—that is, a set of road maps through some key issues. Of course, while these 20 discussion guides cannot possibly cover every issue, they will get you started thinking about curriculum and assessment in a productive way. Like all road maps, they display the options. They do not make the choices. You have to do that. Now, all of the choices, like all roads, have their particular attractions. Whenever you pick one, you may regret the roads not taken. But you do have to choose.

One other point: Few boards make policies on curriculum, and few boards make policies on assessment. Most boards delegate authority over both curriculum and assessment to the professional educators on their staff. (In some cases, the term should not be "delegate," but rather "abandon.") But we believe that civilians—not professional educators—should have the final say about curriculum and assessment. And that is exactly why we wrote this book.

You may learn that your staff members have already made this trip—with or without road maps and with or without board members—and have already made their choices. Maybe they are not the choices you would have made. So you may need to work through those issues again, using the options and arguments provided here in your deliberations as well as other options and arguments your staff members wish to add.

Each discussion guide that follows provides you with a little background on the issue, a few reasonable options, and a few arguments in favor of each option. We have tried hard to keep the reasoning so carefully balanced that the right choice is not obvious. Indeed, there is rarely one choice that is right for all districts. You will have to debate the options and make the choice that is best for your district.

By the way, if you ever want to know what we think, give us a call at 1-800-321-7837. We'll be happy to tell you.

Issue 1: The Board's Point of Entry

Here is one paragraph from a Midwestern board's actual policy:

> The Board shall provide guidance to the Superintendent about each subject field immediately in advance of the beginning of the curriculum development cycle for that subject. The Board shall indicate its position on subject-specific significant issues of curriculum content, such as the emphases to be given to various components of that subject in the elementary, middle, and/or high schools.

This is the policy position of a board that starts even before the curriculum review and revision starts. It wants to provide advance guidance to the curriculum committees of teachers before they begin. It believes that leading the action is better than chasing the action. You may agree.

Or you may prefer to reserve your critique until you have the finished curriculum product in your hands, thinking that you can give a more detailed reaction once you see what the staff is proposing. An intermediate position between starting at the beginning and starting at the end is to call for periodic progress reports as each curriculum committee performs its work. You can ask for those reports to display unresolved issues. That way, you can provide guidance at the forks along the curriculum construction road.

We arrived in one New England town when the board had just refused to approve a new science curriculum that teachers had spent quite some time working on. The board said that it was neither rigorous nor comprehensive enough. The board called for a complete rewriting. The teachers were infuriated and, of course, resented being sent back to the drawing board. The board has yet to recover the respect of those teachers. Now, the board had been absolutely right. The proposed science curriculum was just as the board had characterized it. But at what political cost was the science curriculum rebuilt?

Here are your options (in this case, you may select Option A, B, and/or C in any combination):

Option A ☐ **Express your views before curriculum review and revision begins in a subject.**

- This provides the civilians' point of view about what is important in a subject field before the staff begins its professional work.

- It positions the board to exert its influence before the staff has invested major effort in a product.

- It enables the board to engage in curriculum review without seeming to find fault with the work of the staff.

- It prevents the staff from complaining that they have finished their work and only now is the board providing its input.

Option B ☐ **Express your views as the work proceeds in a subject.**

- This enables the board to monitor the curriculum work, which can help keep it on schedule and within budget.

- It encourages the staff to present curriculum issues to the board as they arise rather than to resolve them without board guidance.

- It enables the board to take corrective action before the product goes too far off track.

- It is arguably easier for the board to do this than to do the initial thinking or to evaluate the final product.

Option C ☐ **Express your views when the work is finished in a subject.**

- This enables the staff to put forward its very best work before the board judges it.

- It saves the board from having to do initial thinking in a subject where board members might not feel qualified.

- It prevents the board from giving the staff unnecessary guidance about what the staff would have done anyway and, thus, saves everyone's time and effort.

- It enables the board to evaluate the curriculum product as a finished whole rather than judging separate, perhaps incomplete, segments of it.

Issue 2: The Curriculum Revision Schedule

How often do you want your curriculum updated—whether that means pruned, expanded, or revised? Should the schedule be the same for all subjects? Or do you think, for example, that mathematics content does not age much in contrast to social studies content, where new events in history and politics call for frequent revision? Do the rules of English grammar (or French or German or Spanish or Latin grammar, for that matter) really change much in contrast to scientific discoveries about space or genetics or nuclear energy or nanotechnology?

What about the schedule for revision at different grades? Can grades K–2 be left alone longer in favor of attending to grades 9–12 more often—or is it the reverse?

Some years ago in a small North Central school district, we overhauled the curriculum in every subject K–12 during one school year. When we left, the curriculum had been thoroughly reviewed and revised by teacher committees under our supervision. The district worried about future revisions, and so did we. We suggested that some type of low-key annual review might suffice inasmuch as such a thorough job had just been completed. District administrators asked teachers to keep notes during the year of any curriculum objectives that they thought should be changed and why. We heard years later that the curriculum was still in place, with the annual reviews being judged by all parties as sufficient. Of course, that works only so long as nothing else big happens—such as new state curriculum standards or a new state testing program with its own requirements or a crisis in district test results.

Recently, we worked for a board in a well-known suburb that was genuinely concerned about the lackluster reading and writing achievement of its students, although they generally came from relatively well-to-do backgrounds and enjoyed many advantages in life. The board had accumulated its dissatisfaction for some years already, but it was not yet time for English to take its turn in the district's multi-year curriculum review and revision cycle. The board decided not to wait any longer. It broke the cycle. It re-scheduled English before its time. It was a good decision for the students, but it disrupted the district's orderly cycle of teacher inservice work and materials purchases and caused considerable irritation among administrators and teachers. Who was right?

Because textbooks historically have been the curriculum containers, the need to adopt new textbooks has become the occasion for curriculum revision. The textbook adoption schedule has become the curriculum revision schedule, the reasoning being that you should not adopt a new textbook until you have reviewed and verified the curriculum it is supposed to deliver. Because textbooks last about five to seven years, most districts have a curriculum revision cycle that is roughly that long, meaning that the math curriculum will be revised and new math textbooks will be bought once every five to seven years. This timetable levels out the costs of curriculum revision and textbook purchasing so that they are about the same from year to year. And it levels out the work of the curriculum director—and probably the elementary school teachers—from year to year.

Here are your options:

Option A ☐ **Call for curriculum review and revision, as needed, in any grade or subject to respond to changing circumstances whenever they occur. Do not adopt a regular schedule.**

- This is a great choice for the students because it keeps the curriculum they are learning as up to date as possible.

- This allows the district to respond immediately to important events, such as the adoption of new state curriculum standards, the development of a new state test, a fall in test scores, a major scientific discovery, or the emergence of a new country.

- This choice means changing the curriculum only when it needs changing—not because it has been a certain number of years and math deserves its turn. In other words, it does not fix what is not broken.

- It might actually reduce the effort and cost of curriculum revision in the long run since changes are made only when necessary.

Option B ☐ **Call for annual curriculum review and revision.**

- This is a great choice for the students and teachers because it updates the curriculum every year. Since the curriculum is updated so often, it never gets too far out of line with what students and teachers need.

- It allows all teachers to participate—with minimal effort—by keeping notes during the year.

- It requires only a small committee in each grade or subject to process teachers' notes at the end of each school year and make whatever changes seem necessary.

- It should reduce the effort and cost of curriculum revision in the long run since annual updates can be done at relatively low cost.

Option C ☐ **Schedule curriculum review and revision on the same cycle as textbook purchases.**

- This is probably the status quo and, therefore, comfortable and familiar to district staff.

- This ensures that systematic attention and equivalent effort will be accorded to all subjects in all grades at their scheduled time and that every subject will get its fair share of new materials.

- It accepts the fact that most teachers are dependent on instructional materials for delivering the curriculum, and so both should be reviewed at the same time.

- It understands that new instructional materials are one reasonable source of curriculum objectives; thus, it makes sense for teachers to examine such materials when considering curriculum changes.

Issue 3: An Obligation or Option for Teachers

Some teachers treat published district curriculum objectives as an obligation, as something they must teach, and they worry when they do not get them all taught. But, many teachers treat published district curriculum objectives rather as suggestions about what they might teach—not as something they must teach—even if they were on the committee that developed the objectives. Oftentimes, teachers in the same district hold these two different views. When your district establishes curriculum objectives, you need to be clear on which view you expect your teachers to take.

Recently, we attended the annual kick-off PTA meeting at a large urban high school of 4,000 students. The assistant principal who supervised the English Department described the English curriculum to the parents assembled:

> "Our English teachers will be following the State standards, and we'll be working on helping our students meet those standards in reading and writing. Of course, as you may know, the standards are quite general as to what students must accomplish in high school. After working on the standards, our teachers are pretty much free to teach whatever they wish and to use their creativity in the classroom."

This statement is not unusual. It results from a widely held view among educators that each individual teacher should be not only free, but also encouraged, to decide the content of the curriculum, taking into consideration the ability and interests of the students, the available instructional materials, and the teacher's own background, training, and interests. Some say that having such freedom is the mark of a respected professional in the field of education.

The model for this is the highly skilled, semi-independent university graduate school research professor, whose courses are made up partly—or even largely—of the professor's own interests and discoveries. You will have to decide how much of the graduate school model is applicable to your elementary and secondary schools.

Here are your options:

Option A ☐ **Leave the curriculum objectives to the choice of the individual teachers.**

- This is highly acceptable to teachers.

- It makes the best use of the special knowledge and training of each teacher.

- It does not ask teachers to teach material that they have not been trained to teach or material that they themselves do not enjoy. (It prevents comments like this one that an eleventh grade English teacher made recently at the start of a new school year: "This year, one of the books that we will be reading is *The Red Badge of Courage*. I read this book a long time ago when I was a student and didn't like it. I recently tried to re-read it and couldn't even get through it this time.")

Option B ☐ **Obligate all teachers to teach board-established curriculum objectives for part of the year, leaving them free to teach what they wish the remainder of the time.**

- This is a compromise that is relatively acceptable to teachers—depending on the results of a necessary debate at the board table about what percentage of the year the board-established objectives will occupy and what percentage of the year will be left for the teacher-established objectives.

- It guarantees students a common curriculum of essential material, including whatever State suggestions or requirements there might be, regardless of which teachers they have.

- It allows some freedom for teachers to make use of their special knowledge, interests, and backgrounds.

Option C ☐ **Obligate all teachers to teach board-established curriculum objectives that are rigorous and challenging enough to occupy the whole school year.**

- This will be objectionable at first to many teachers, although not necessarily unacceptable to them in the end.

- This guarantees all students a rigorous and challenging curriculum, regardless of which teachers they have, and it guarantees parents and taxpayers the most substantial curriculum the board can establish for all students.

- It requires the teachers and administrators to produce an outstanding curriculum—inasmuch as the district will be committing students to it for some 180 days—and it requires the board to use very high standards in judging that curriculum before adopting it.

Issue 4: State Curriculum Standards as a Source of Curriculum Objectives

In recent years, most states have tried hard to produce curriculum "standards"—that is, statements of what students should learn—that are rigorous and comprehensive, but that allow for enough local control to make those standards acceptable to all districts. In other words, state standards usually leave enough room for districts to make a reasonably wide range of curriculum choices within the broader state standards. Many states have incorporated the recommendations of various national curriculum commissions into their own standards—such as the standards produced by the National Council of Teachers of Mathematics and the National Standards for Arts Education, produced by a consortium of four national arts education associations. But no state has done a perfect job of making its standards in all subjects both rigorous and comprehensive. We can see that by comparing the work of various states.

In some states in some subjects, state curriculum standards specify what students are required to learn—and, in fact, students may be tested by the state to see that they have learned it. In other states, state curriculum standards are closer to recommendations about what students should learn. In those cases, districts have more options. You will need to discuss the relationship of your district's curriculum objectives to your state's curriculum standards. You may want to teach more than your state requires or recommends, calling for your district's curriculum objectives to be more rigorous or comprehensive than your state's standards. But should you? And in some states, you may want or need to teach less than your state requires or recommends. But should you?

Before you make any decision on this topic, you need to know what is in your state's standards. For example, if you were in one New England state, you would need to know that your state's art standards call for a curriculum that includes a heavy dose of art history and multicultural art appreciation every year K–8. Or, if you were in one Midwestern state, you would need to know that your state's English standards call for viewing skills (e.g., making informed judgments about television news programs, reviewing film documentaries, analyzing posters and graphic advertisements), starting in the primary grades—to go along with the more traditional reading, writing, speaking, and listening skills. Or, if you were in one Southwestern state, you would need to know that your state's social studies standards call for a curriculum that teaches attitudes—not just knowledge—about democracy and about free enterprise. How could you judge your own district's curriculum without knowing your own state's standards in each subject?

There really is no substitute for examining your own state's standards for yourself. Of course, you can and should listen to the explanations and opinions of administrators and teachers in your own district as well as of outside experts. But, sooner or later, you will need to develop your own opinion about whether your district's curriculum objectives should be more challenging than the state's standards. It might be one of the most important and influential judgments you will make as a board member.

One more thing to remember: Many state curriculum standards are not specific enough to be used as district objectives themselves. Many times, they are not even allocated to single grades, but rather cover a span of grades (say, K–2 or 5–8); those would have to be broken down by grade before teachers could use them in their classrooms. (We might say that state standards often function as goals—that is, the more general statements of student learning that set the stage for the more specific curriculum objectives to be written and adopted by local districts.)

In a number of states, we have translated state curriculum standards into curriculum objectives that can be used more easily by classroom teachers. This kind of translation is something that your teachers will have to do for themselves. But do not expect them to be able to do it quickly. It is a tedious and exacting process.

Here are your options (you might want to use a combination, depending on the grade and subject):

Option A ☐ **Use your state's curriculum standards, whenever possible, as your district's curriculum objectives.**

- This trusts and respects what the state has ordered.

- This will not strain your district financially in an attempt to go beyond what the state has declared as its minimums.

- This will leave plenty of room for teachers to make their own curriculum choices within state standards since state standards are typically broader than what we think of as curriculum objectives.

- This will help students do well on state tests since teachers can spend their time focused on the state curriculum.

Option B ☐ **Adopt your state's curriculum standards as the framework for your district's curriculum objectives, but make your objectives clearer and more specific.**

- This keeps your curriculum objectives within the boundaries outlined by the state.

- This translates the state curriculum standards into objectives that are explicit enough to assign to individual grades.

- This translates the state curriculum standards into objectives that are explicit enough to guide lesson planning—something the state probably has not done for districts, but something that your teachers will eventually have to do for themselves.

- This translates the state curriculum standards into objectives that are explicit and narrow enough to let your own teachers develop local tests to match.

Option C ☐ **Use your state's curriculum standards, but go beyond them when developing your district's curriculum objectives, adding content from other sources.**

- This uses what your state has done, but makes up for any gaps that it inadvertently left when it was doing its work.

- This takes advantage of ideas from outside the state, making your curriculum objectives more comprehensive and perhaps more balanced than the state's.

- This takes advantage of ideas from inside the district, making your curriculum objectives more appropriate to your own local situation and perhaps more innovative than the state's.

- This assures students of learning beyond what is probably average in your state.

Issue 5: Other Sources of Curriculum Objectives

Curriculum objectives are the building blocks of your district curriculum. Where do you want your teachers and administrators to obtain building blocks to supplement those mandated or recommended in your state curriculum standards? Or do you even want them supplemented?

Understandably, left to their own devices, curriculum committees of teachers will tend to use only two sources: (1) their own personal backgrounds, interests, and experiences; and (2) their current or past instructional materials. Understandably, they will seldom propose to teach what they themselves do not know or to teach topics without suitable textbooks or other materials.

Working in a New England district recently with outstanding art teachers, we had a discussion of ceramics objectives for the elementary schools. A number of those art teachers did not have much experience in ceramics themselves and did not, at that time, have the equipment for teaching ceramics. But should ceramics be taught? They all agreed it should. But did they want to step forward in uncertain times with inadequate budgets and inadequate experience to take it on? Listening to the teachers, we could hear those topics being debated. The board, unfortunately, was not present.

If you want your teachers to cast a net wider than their own experience, you will have to point toward the ocean. There are many sources of objectives out there in addition to your state's curriculum standards: national curriculum commission reports and standards, nationally standardized tests, state tests, the curricula of admirable school districts in your state or outside your state, instructional materials not used in your district, "banks" of curriculum objectives from various sources, specialized courses such as Advanced Placement courses, and so on.

You may find that your teachers are not savvy about all of these sources. We have even found that a surprising number of teachers are not familiar with their own state's curriculum standards. Talking to a group of about 30 K–8 language arts teachers and looking over the curriculum objectives that they had been working on, we asked why they had covered only about half of the state's curriculum standards. They said that they were not familiar with the state standards and, thus, had not used them in producing their work. They asked whether we might do that for them. That was several years ago, and we would like to believe that districts are doing a better job of using state standards than they once did. But, if we were you, we wouldn't simply count on it. If teachers are unfamiliar with their own state's work, they probably know even less about other sources of objectives. That is a serious matter.

Of course, the sources of objectives that your teachers use can ultimately determine the quality of your own district's objectives. You will want the quality to be exemplary, and thus you are likely to want multiple sources used.

Here are your options (you will certainly want to use a combination of these options—perhaps different combinations for various subjects and grades—to produce a well-rounded product):

Option A ☐ **Call for national commission recommendations and standards to be reviewed.**

- This enables your district to move beyond state requirements and to fill in any gaps left in your state's work.

Option B ☐ **Call for nationally standardized tests to be reviewed.**

- This assures the board that whatever is tested in a variety of national tests (not just the ones you use) will not be overlooked and may appear in your curriculum objectives. This includes both tests provided by major commercial test publishers and tests produced by not-for-profit organizations, such as the National Assessment of Educational Progress.

Option C ☐ **Call for state tests to be reviewed.**

- Since state tests are not always a perfect match to the state's curriculum standards, this assures the board that whatever is in the state tests will appear in the district curriculum objectives.

Option D ☐ **Call for a variety of instructional materials—including, but not limited to, textbooks—to be reviewed.**

- This ensures that teachers and any curriculum specialists go beyond what they are accustomed to and assures the board that appropriate instructional materials would be available to teach whatever objectives might be proposed.

Option E ☐ **Call for other school districts' curriculum objectives to be reviewed.**

- This takes advantage of the work of other talented district staffs—broadening the perspective of your own staff members, while being economically efficient.

Option F ☐ **Call for selected other states' curriculum standards to be reviewed.**

- This takes advantage of the work of other talented states (but remember that states differ radically in the quality of their work).

Option G ☐ **Call for your own district teachers and administrators to be consulted.**

- This assures that the diverse backgrounds and experiences of your own classroom teachers and any curriculum specialists—as well as their unique understanding of your students—are brought to bear on your curriculum objectives.

Issue 6: Difficulty of the Objectives

All curriculum committees, sooner or later, consciously or unconsciously, have to answer this question: "How hard should the curriculum objectives be?" In practice, this means, "What percent of the students can be expected to learn these in one school year, given adequate teaching?"

The simplest and most powerful attack against a test is to say that too many students fail it. The same applies to a set of curriculum objectives. They cannot be too hard for students. But, they must be hard enough. What is too hard and what is too easy? Let's try to use common sense to get the answer.

We were working one time with some elementary school music teachers in a college town in a North Central state. Looking at their draft objectives for each grade, it was clear that their graduating fifth graders could play in a symphony orchestra and, even more impressively, compose the music for one. These objectives must have been written for the best music students the teachers had ever had or, in some cases, could ever have imagined. Obviously, they were too hard for most students—dazzling, but unrealistic.

On the other hand, if the objectives had been written so that every student could have learned them, including the least talented student in each grade, they would have been too easy for many students—not sufficiently challenging and, therefore, boring to many. In that same North Central college town, we once tested third grade students on a sample of their third grade objectives right at the beginning of the school year. They did remarkably well on the test—even before they had been taught the objectives. The conclusion was obvious: The objectives were too easy for many students. In our experience, teachers are more likely to make the objectives too easy rather than too hard. So, you will need to give policy guidance about finding some middle ground.

But any middle ground will leave the curriculum too hard for some students. What can be done for them? All possible solutions have one characteristic in common: more time. That is, they require the student to spend extra time working to learn the curriculum. Whether it is summer school classes or tutoring after school or remediation during the school day, the student will need to spend extra time. How much of that time can the district pay for? You need to keep the answer in mind when you are deciding how high your expectations should be.

Here are your options (of course, you may apply the same kind of reasoning as displayed in Option A, B, and/or C, but invent an option of your own that targets a different percentage of students):

Option A ☐ Design the curriculum objectives so that about 70 percent of your students can learn them on a normal schedule.

- This makes for an extremely challenging curriculum that expects a lot from students. It sets your expectations as high as probably would be reasonable.

- It gives most students excellent preparation for the next grade.

- It prepares most students to do well on state and national tests.

Option B ☐ **Design the curriculum objectives so that about 80 percent of your students can learn them on a normal schedule.**

- This makes for a challenging curriculum that expects a lot from students.

- It is likely to be acceptable to teachers when they consider that they must teach the curriculum successfully to 4 out of 5 students in their classroom.

- It reduces the number of students who need extra help and, thus, saves the district money.

Option C ☐ **Design the curriculum objectives so that about 90 percent of your students can learn them on a normal schedule.**

- This makes for a less challenging curriculum and, thus, reduces still further the number of students who will need extra help.

- It reduces the number of complaints from parents and students about a curriculum that is too difficult for some students.

- It makes the schools look more effective to parents and the public by ensuring that more students will achieve what is expected of them.

Issue 7: Affective Objectives

Pardon the jargon. *Affect* means *feelings*; affective objectives include interests, attitudes, appreciations, and values. You may have heard educators speak of "Bloom's taxonomy": that is, a classification of the levels of thinking—from simple recall to complex evaluative and critical thinking. Identified by Benjamin Bloom and his committee of researchers 50 years ago, this "cognitive taxonomy" has been widely used to develop curriculum objectives ever since.

Well, there was also a classification of the levels of feeling, published almost 10 years later as the "affective taxonomy," by David Krathwohl and his committee of researchers. It never got as much press as Bloom's taxonomy, but it is equally appropriate for educators to use. Do you want your staff to use it?

Simply put, the question is this: Do you teach students how to feel? Your automatic answer might be this: "Of course we do not teach students how to feel. We educate them. We do not indoctrinate them." Well, pause and think again. Do you teach them to love their country? Respect other cultures? Appreciate art? Enjoy music? Read for pleasure? Accept children of other races? Be good sports? Take turns? Be honest? All of those—and many others—are more a matter of feeling right than thinking right. So if you teach those, you are teaching affective objectives.

Consequently, you will have to take thought—and guide your teachers as they create curriculum objectives—about whether and what you will teach students to feel: about their community, their state, regular exercise, drug use, proper diet, poetry, plagiarism, the inventiveness of scientists, the law, the politically oppressed, and so on.

Some people feel that developing good feelings in children is just as important as developing good thinking. One reason is that they believe that feelings affect learning. In fact, research shows that students' attitudes toward the study of science and math are set for life by the time students are in second grade. In other words, if those very young students do not find science and math to be engaging and interesting, if they are not curious enough to do experiments to see what happens, if they don't enjoy solving math puzzles, then they will likely not want to pursue the study of science and math beyond what is required of them. We once wrote a K–8 math curriculum for a Southern city in which affective objectives were carefully included in every grade in an effort to improve students' attitudes toward—and hopefully achievement in—math. Was that what you would have required? When was the last time your board discussed students' feelings about math with a curriculum committee?

Here are your options:

Option A ☐ **Include affective objectives in every grade and subject.**

- This recognizes that students will inevitably develop attitudes toward every subject and feelings about issues in every subject, and it attempts to guide them.

- It recognizes that attitudes affect willingness to learn a subject.

- It encourages teachers to express enthusiasm for their subjects and to make an effort to share that enthusiasm with their students.

Option B ☐ **Include affective objectives in selected grades and subjects.**

- This recognizes that some subjects—such as art, music, and physical education—might lend themselves to the cultivation of attitudes better than others.

- It recognizes that favorable attitudes toward subjects that become elective at some point in high school (such as art, music, science, foreign languages) are critical to maintaining enrollment in those subjects.

- Teachers of some subjects may resist the inclusion of attitudes in their curriculum.

Option C ☐ **Do not include affective objectives in any grade or subject.**

- This recognizes that students' attitudes toward a subject and toward its content will be affected by many circumstances and that they can't be guided easily.

- It recognizes that attitudes toward any subject will differ dramatically among students in a classroom and that those attitudes can't be expected to be the same.

- It accepts the fact that some educators and some parents do not believe that it is the school's place to impart values to students.

Issue 8: Teaching Schedule for the Objectives

You have to decide whether to give teachers a full school year to teach the set of curriculum objectives for a subject or to have the objectives divided into segments— either semesters or marking periods. Of course, board members will not actually divide the objectives into semesters or marking periods. You will simply call for the curriculum committees of teachers to do so before they propose objectives to you for approval.

In deciding whether to call for that division of objectives, one consideration is whether you want district-developed tests that can tell you whether students are learning the objectives and, if so, how often you want to get those test results. If once-a-year test results are enough, you don't need a teaching schedule for the objectives. Give teachers the whole year. Let each individual teacher teach them at any rate and in any sequence he or she chooses. On the other hand, if you don't want to wait until the end of the year for test results, you will have to schedule the objectives to fit a more frequent testing schedule. (More about this in a later discussion guide.)

Another consideration is when your state administers its tests. Should the curriculum be sequenced so that the objectives tested by the state are scheduled to be taught in your classrooms before your students take any state tests?

Yet another consideration is whether your teachers share materials, such as classroom sets of novels or science kits, exchanging them during the year so that *The Great Gatsby* or magnets get taught in September by one teacher and in May by another. That kind of sharing argues against adopting any kind of schedule for teaching the objectives.

There are always dominoes that fall, sometimes unpredictably. Recently, in one suburban New England district, the teachers lobbied successfully not to divide up the English objectives, but rather to allow the whole year for teaching them. That decision caused all of the district-developed English tests required by the board to be given at the end of the school year. Because the district testing program included several English tests for each grade (e.g., nonfiction, short fiction, long fiction, poetry), it turned out to be a lot of testing in a short time frame. Could there have been a compromise?

Here are your options (you may decide to use one option for some grades and/or subjects and another option for others):

Option A ☐ Do not schedule the teaching of objectives.

- This option will be the most popular choice with teachers and will lessen their resistance to having to teach the objectives at all.

- This frees individual teachers to employ the teaching sequence that works best for their own students and to be creative in grouping objectives into units of their own design.

- It gives teachers a full year to get the job done (rather than interrupting them with artificial deadlines).

- It enables teachers to take turns using materials that are in limited supply so that their use can be spread throughout the school year.

- This gives teachers the best chance for re-teaching what students did not learn adequately the first time.

Option B ☐ **Schedule the teaching of objectives by semester.**

- This gives individual teachers sufficient elbow room for sequencing objectives within the semester to fit their personal preferences or their students' abilities.

- It enables individual teachers or, indeed, grade levels or departments to base semester final exams (even common final exams) directly on the objectives assigned to that semester.

- It gives teachers a mid-point verification that their teaching is on schedule—and leaves ample time for catching up if it is not.

- This permits the board to give parents some idea of what is being taught when.

- This permits the board to schedule mid-year testing, if it chooses to do so, thus preventing end-of-year district tests that are too long and take up too much time in the last few weeks of school.

Option C ☐ **Schedule the teaching of objectives by marking period.**

- This gives teachers even better notice as to whether their teaching is on schedule—which is especially helpful to inexperienced teachers and to teachers new to the district.

- It enables teachers to base their own marking-period final exams directly on the objectives assigned to that marking period (which may make the exams seem fairer in the eyes of students).

- It makes it easier for principals and/or central office specialists to supervise teachers.

- This permits the board to give parents an even better idea of what is being taught when.

- This permits the board to schedule testing at the end of each marking period, if it chooses to do so, thus preventing end-of-semester or end-of-year district tests that are too long and take up too much time.

Issue 9: Guiding Instruction

Curriculum is the *what* of learning. *Instruction* is the *how* of teaching. We bring up instruction because it is sometimes entangled—and often confused—with curriculum. To what degree, if at all, do you want to guide the choice of teaching methods in your classrooms?

You might say, "So long as our curriculum gets taught, we don't care how it gets taught." Some boards have made that deal with their teachers. In other words, once the board has adopted the curriculum objectives, teachers are free to use whatever teaching methods they prefer. That is a reasonable position since we don't believe that board members themselves know enough to guide teaching methods. Teaching methods are a matter of professional training and professional judgment. In fact, we see time and time again that teachers are much better at planning instruction (and carrying it out) than at planning curriculum.

Sometimes administrators intercede between the board and the teachers to guide or even dictate instruction in the classroom. We know an urban district where administrators required reading teachers to arrange the students on a rug in a semicircle while the teacher sat in a rocking chair, to use certain colors of paper for bulletin board displays, and to use a specified number of staples when mounting papers. To what degree should administrators be allowed to control the instructional methods of your teachers? That is a policy issue for board members to decide: Who has the final say about the teaching methods?

Sometimes the textbooks and other materials guide or even dictate instruction in the classroom. The ubiquitous hands-on science kits now used in thousands of elementary school classrooms are, in effect, a method of instruction. They include not only what science is to be taught, but also how that science is to be taught (in this case, through hands-on activities and experiments). Interestingly, these kits are better at guiding science instruction than they are at building a science curriculum because, typically, too few kits are used in a year to make up a comprehensive curriculum.

By the way, some people think that instruction is more important than curriculum. "It doesn't matter how good the curriculum is if the teacher can't teach it," they say. More tellingly, they argue, "Children will forget almost everything they learn in school," (that is, they will forget the curriculum). "But a good teacher will teach children how to learn, and that's what they'll remember. So good instruction is more important than good curriculum." You will want to consider that as you decide how far to go in guiding instruction.

Here are your options:

Option A ☐ **Require the uniform use of good teaching practices identified by the administration.**

- This obligates the administration to seek and find and communicate successful teaching practices to teachers—and further obligates the administration to enforce the use of those practices.

- It guarantees every student the best teaching the profession can invent.

- It assures parents that their children will get good teaching, no matter who the teacher is.

- This will probably become acceptable to the majority of teachers over time, even though it will be met with serious resistance initially.

Option B ☐ **Recommend that teachers use good teaching practices identified by the administration.**

- This obligates the administration to seek and find successful teaching practices.

- It further obligates the administration to find and use persuasive ways of displaying these practices to teachers, but prevents administrators from getting carried away in requiring teachers to do things a certain way in the classroom.

- It frees teachers to use other teaching methods whenever they prefer to do so.

- This will be acceptable to most teachers immediately.

Option C ☐ **Free teachers to select any teaching practices they wish.**

- This encourages teachers to draw on their own training and experience and to adapt their teaching methods to the particular students in their classes.

- It recognizes that the profession has had great difficulty in identifying certain teaching methods as being superior to others.

- It admits that it is almost impossible to monitor the methods that teachers are using in the classroom and, therefore, saves the efforts of administrators in trying.

- This will be strongly endorsed by most teachers.

Issue 10: Communication to Parents

Most school districts are better at telling parents what children will be having for lunch than they are at describing what they will be taught during the rest of the day. Even districts that have well-established board-approved curriculum objectives rarely communicate those objectives to parents.

Some board members, administrators, and teachers believe that too few parents have enough time or interest or education to pay attention to what the schools are teaching—especially in the upper grades. Others believe that an appreciable fraction of parents do have the time and interest and education not only to pay attention to the curriculum, but also to help their children learn it—especially in the lower grades.

Sometimes parents surprise you. One time we were working in an urban county in the Southeast, and we had just redone the curriculum K–8 in English, math, science, social studies, and health. The new superintendent decided to send the entire set of curriculum objectives home to parents for the grades their children were in. He had them formatted as a checklist. And, he had to break them down into marking periods because there were a lot of objectives and he did not want the checklists to be overwhelming for parents.

Everyone told him that he was wasting money. Many parents would not even be able to read the objectives he was sending home, they said. But he persisted for a year.

The next fall when the new school year started, the district was late sending parents their copies of what came to be known as the "parent checklists." Principals around town reported that their phones were ringing off the hook, with parents saying, "Where is my checklist? How do you expect me to help my child this year when you haven't sent my checklist?"

Was the superintendent right? More important, how would parents in your district react? How many parents in your district would actually make any use of such curriculum checklists? 50 percent? 25 percent? 10 percent? If even 10 percent of your parents used the checklists to work with their children, would learning improve in your district? When was the last time your board discussed that with your superintendent?

Here are your options (you can, of course, select different options for different grades and/or subjects):

Option A ☐ **Do not communicate curriculum objectives to parents.**

- This is the least expensive choice and administratively the simplest.

- It avoids sending unnecessary—or even unwanted—materials to parents, thus avoiding complaints about wasting taxpayers' money on printing and mailing.

- Many teachers will support this option—especially those who don't want aggressive parents looking over their shoulders.

Option B ☐ **Send brief summaries of curriculum objectives for a child's grade or subjects to parents.**

- This gives interested parents an overview of the curriculum, without giving disinterested parents more information than they want and can use.

- This will tend to stabilize the curriculum within the boundaries described in the summary, thus helping to assure that some common things will be taught to children by all teachers in a grade or subject.

- This is what many districts do now, so it is probably a reasonable balance of what is useful to parents, what is cost-effective for the district, and what is acceptable to teachers.

Option C ☐ **Send the complete set of curriculum objectives for a child's grade or subjects to parents.**

- This gives parents the same objectives teachers have and enables interested parents to help their children learn those objectives.

- This is an unusually effective and relatively inexpensive way to make sure that the curriculum, as planned, actually gets taught behind the classroom door.

- Some teachers will actually support this option (though quietly) because they believe that some of their colleagues are not teaching everything that is expected of them.

Issue 11: National, State, and District Tests

There are three kinds of tests:

1. *Optional nationally standardized tests made, distributed, and (usually) scored by commercial publishers.* They are "national" in that they are sold nationwide. They are "standardized" as to the testing conditions, such as the time allowed for taking them, so that the scores can be compared for all students taking the tests nationwide. You do not have to use any of these tests, but many districts elect to do so.

2. *Mandatory state tests made, distributed, and (usually) scored by the state* (They are also "standardized," for the same reason as the national tests and, just to make things more complicated, some states purchase both their tests and their scoring services from commercial publishers of nationally standardized tests.) State tests are based on your state's required curriculum—typically in English and math, often in science and social studies, but rarely in other subjects. Of course, you have to use these mandatory state tests. Occasionally, a state will designate a test as optional or will require tests in benchmark grades and make optional tests in the same subject available for the in-between grades.

3. *Optional district tests created, administered, and scored by your own district.* (The conditions for them should, of course, be "standardized" as well so that the results will be comparable from year to year and student to student.) Naturally, you would base these tests squarely on your own district's curriculum (which would necessarily include the state's curriculum)—the best defense against teachers' customary attack that "the tests do not match what we teach."

Let's talk about state's curriculum for a minute. About two decades ago, more and more states started taking over more and more control of the curriculum. We often say to board members in workshops, "Where were you? The states waited for you to do what needed to be done—to set forth a clear, comprehensive, and challenging curriculum for your students. And when so many of you did not do it, the states were forced to. Forced by legislatures, which got forced by complaining parents and employers."

And so more recently with state tests—albeit with some states now being pushed by federal complaints. We could just as easily say, "Where were you, board members? The states waited and waited for you to do what needed to be done—to require the use of clear, comprehensive, and challenging tests to show how your students were doing in school. And most of you didn't." Consequently, states began creating batteries of tests to prove whether your students were learning.

Not surprisingly, there are a lot of complaints about state tests and how they are used. Many of the complaints come from professional educators, and some are well deserved. But every once in a while they come from local board members. Don't complain, we would say. You had your chance.

And so, now you will give whatever tests are required by your state to meet its self-imposed or federally imposed testing requirements. But you still have the following options (you can, of course, select different options or a combination of options for different grades and/or subjects):

Option A ☐ **Use nationally standardized tests made and distributed by commercial publishers.**

- This is your only way to compare your students to students across the country.

- These tests are reasonably efficient to administer and score, requiring just a handful of hours of testing time a year for each student and a reasonable per-student scoring fee.

- They have credibility with parents and the public, though less with educators.

- They can provide reasonably good trend data from year to year, showing ups and downs in student achievement over time.

Option B ☐ **Use both mandatory and optional state tests to judge learning whenever possible.**

- This takes full advantage of what your state has spent a lot of money doing, and it is the lowest-cost option for your district.

- This causes students to be tested on what the state has set forth in its curriculum standards and what you, therefore, have included in your local curriculum standards.

- These tests have credibility with parents and the public, though less with educators—and less with parents and the public if there has been negative press in your state about the tests themselves and/or a high failure rate among students.

- They, too, can provide reasonably good trend data from year to year, showing ups and downs in student achievement over time— although state tests may not be as consistent from year to year as nationally standardized tests are.

Option C ☐ **Create and use your own district tests in an array of grades and subjects.**

- This is likely to be most acceptable to your teachers, especially if they have a hand in creating the tests—but do not expect teachers as a group to praise the idea of district tests.

- This gives your district maximum flexibility in what and when to test—although it is likely to be the most expensive of the testing options, given what it will cost to create, pilot test, administer, and score an array of valid and reliable tests.

- These tests will be an excellent match for the curriculum that is actually being taught in your classrooms and can test subjects that national and state tests rarely address, such as art and music.

- These tests can eventually provide reasonably good trend data, showing ups and downs in student achievement from year to year.

41

Issue 12: The Amount of Testing Time

"Too much testing" is a common complaint among teachers—sometimes echoed by parents. It is an interesting complaint because, looking at the school year as a whole, almost all of the tests that students have to take are tests created by their own teachers and given by their teachers at their own discretion, without any direction from any administrator in the school or in the district..

Let's look at the numbers. The school year contains a little over 1,000 clock hours: 6 hours per day for 185 days = 1,110 hours. In some grades in some states, mandatory state tests take up perhaps 20 hours, or about 2 percent of the year. But in some states in some grades, state testing time is considerably less, sometimes nonexistent.

The nationally standardized tests required by many school boards take up perhaps another 20 hours, or another approximately 2 percent of the year. But in some districts in some grades, testing time for nationally standardized tests is considerably less, often nonexistent.

So, even in the most-tested grades in the most-tested districts, about 96 percent of classroom time is left untouched by "outside" testing. If you adopted a comprehensive program of district-created tests matching your district curriculum in *all* grades and *all* subjects (an extremely unlikely occurrence), those tests would take perhaps another 20 to 40 hours for each child, or another 2 to 4 percent of each child's year. In the most extreme testing case, about 92 percent of any child's time would be left untouched by the testing program established by the state and the board.

As a matter of fact, it is the psychological strain of "outside" testing and reporting of results that causes many teachers and indeed many administrators and some parents to complain—not the time students spend actually taking the tests. And it might be the time that some teachers and administrators devote to giving students practice tests and other test preparation assignments that eats into the teachers' instructional time—again, not the time students spend actually taking the tests. Every professional has a horror story about that. In some states, preparation for the state tests is legendary—and not in a good way. In one top-notch suburban district we worked in, we discovered that the middle school teachers in a variety of subjects drilled the students on mathematics for a couple of weeks in preparation for the state test in the fall. You should understand all of that in adopting your testing policy.

Here are some options for you:

Option A ☐ **Accept the state's testing time as being enough for the district.**

- This choice—doing what the state requires, but nothing more—lets you escape responsibility for all of the complaints about testing time. Complainants would have to blame the state.

- It trusts the state to evaluate and report on student learning in the district—to students, teachers, parents, the public, and the board—in whatever grades and subjects the state chooses to test.

- It saves instructional time for teachers to use to better effect than giving more tests than the state requires.

Option B ☐ **Adopt a fixed amount of time for each grade or selected grades that can be used each year for any board-required evaluation (including both nationally standardized tests and any district-created tests).**

- This choice gives a clear message that you are concerned about student achievement and that you believe that testing is one way to get useful evidence.

- It requires you to give systematic attention to the testing time issue, deal with all concerns, and reach a firm decision that can be communicated to all interested parties.

- It gives the superintendent careful guidance in the design of a testing program and allows enough time for tests to be purchased or developed prior to administration.

Option C ☐ **Allow testing time for board-required evaluation (including both nationally standardized tests and any district-created tests) to vary from year to year, according to the board's interests.**

- This choice gives you maximum flexibility in evaluating student achievement—though that flexibility might unnerve the administrators and teachers to some degree.

- It shows that you consider carefully what to test at any given time rather than simply adhering to the same testing schedule year after year.

- It avoids a testing-time quota that you or your administrators might feel obligated to fill.

Issue 13: Types of Assessments
for Measuring and Judging Learning

During the last several decades, professional educators have created a panoply of assessment tools and techniques. Some of the most recent developments have been stimulated by opposition to paper-and-pencil tests that had traditionally consisted largely of multiple-choice test questions. Although judging student performances, products, and portfolios has been championed as a superior method of assessment, traditional paper-and-pencil tests continue to predominate, partly because of their relatively wider subject-matter coverage, shorter testing time, quicker scoring, and lower cost.

If you are going to have district tests, you need to consider when to make them traditional paper-and-pencil tests and when to make them nontraditional tests. Here are some examples of when to use nontraditional tests:

- *Performance tests* may be best for occasions when students actually perform without paper and pencil: violin solos, theater productions, relay races, persuasive speeches, automobile tune-ups, science experiments.

- *Product tests* may be best for occasions when students actually create products: computer programs, birdhouses, poems, clay sculptures, relief maps of the U.S., models of the solar system.

- *Portfolios* may be best for occasions when it is important to evaluate the evolution of students' skills over time as well as the different types of products students have created: a collection of nonfiction essays, a collection of paintings, a collection of musical compositions.

Evaluating performance tests, product tests, and portfolios requires judgments to be made by an expert observer—ideally, by more than one expert observer. It requires identifying both a set of characteristics on which to judge the performance or product or portfolio and appropriate scales to show to what degree each characteristic is evident (these are often called "rubrics"). Ideally, it requires real performances or products at each point on the scale, against which observers can judge the students' work—for example, actual clay pots or tapes of trumpet solos exemplifying five different levels of achievement. Finally, it requires that multiple expert observers practice judging together for a while until they are using roughly the same standards for making their judgments.

Of course, it takes time to make and consolidate such judgments. But even if one teacher is judging her own students' models of a Native American longhouse, it takes more time than grading a traditional paper-and-pencil test. All of this is why it is more time consuming and more expensive to use these alternative forms of assessment.

We have often said to school districts, "Measure when you can; judge when you can't." In other words, use traditional paper-and-pencil tests when you can, and use alternative methods when you can't. But what will you do?

Here are your options:

Option A ☐ **Express a preference for using traditional paper-and-pencil tests.**

- This gives you the several advantages of traditional tests: relatively wider subject-matter coverage, shorter testing time, quicker scoring, and lower cost.

- This provides more consistent—and perhaps fairer—scoring than can be easily achieved through using rubrics to judge student performances, products, and portfolios.

- This may yield test results that are more credible—or, at least, more familiar—to the board, parents, and general public than non-traditional tests might provide.

Option B ☐ **Express a preference for using students' performances, products, and portfolios.**

- This places the district on the frontier of assessment methodology.

- This opens often overlooked subjects—like art and music and physical education—to more systematic evaluation (since nontraditional assessments are often a better fit for those subjects), and it also demonstrates your interest in those subjects.

- This will be interesting for many teachers, though they will need to dedicate additional time and effort in order to administer and score such tests.

Option C ☐ **Express a preference for using a mix of both traditional paper-and-pencil tests and students' performances, products, and portfolios, depending on which assessments are most appropriate for any given subject or grade.**

- This is designed to get the most valuable information, though not necessarily at the lowest cost.

- This both frees and challenges the professional staff to seek and find—or to create—the best type of assessment for each subject and grade.

- It has all the positives—as well as all the negatives—of the other options.

Issue 14: Types of Questions in Traditional Paper-and-Pencil District Tests

Most educators believe that open-ended questions (sometimes called "constructed response" questions) are better than multiple-choice questions for determining what students have learned. They believe that things like creativity, orderly reasoning, and effective presentation skills—all of which are extremely important—cannot be measured by multiple-choice questions. So they favor open-ended questions in which the student has to construct the right answer rather than choose it from a list.

But some testing experts disagree, arguing that good multiple-choice questions work well enough as a sample of what students know—and take much less time to administer and much less money to score. Moreover, they say, students will meet multiple-choice questions in many tests they will need to take in their futures, including those for college admission.

Interestingly, classroom teachers have always used open-ended questions in the tests they make up for their own students: fill-in-the-blanks, short answers, and multi-paragraph essays. Such questions are actually much easier for test developers to write, although they are much harder to score—especially the longer essays. Some testing experts would argue that teachers, who are not typically trained either in college or in staff development sessions to write good multiple-choice questions, are probably better off sticking to open-ended questions.

But that does not answer the question: What kinds of questions should you call for on any traditional paper-and-pencil district tests you will give to measure your students' achievement: open-ended, multiple-choice, or both?

We should note, in passing, that open-ended questions are harder for students, requiring both more effort and more time from them. Accordingly, more classroom time must be allocated to testing, which teachers will complain about. Teachers might also complain about having to score their own students' answers—or even the answers of other students in the school—without additional time or compensation for doing it.

Of course, teachers will complain about multiple-choice questions as well, just for different reasons. They will be concerned that multiple-choice questions are trivial or purposely tricky, have unnecessarily difficult vocabulary in them, or cannot be finished in the time allotted. And, some of the time, they will be right.

There is another consideration. In the past decade, states have begun to adopt both short open-ended questions and multi-paragraph essays for use in state tests. The inclusion of such questions has helped make state tests more acceptable to educators—though more expensive for states to score and more formidable for students. Including the same kinds of questions in district tests can help students practice for those kinds of questions in the state tests.

Here are your options:

Option A ☐ **Use only open-ended questions in district tests.**

- This will be acceptable to most teachers and to all parents.

- This allows district staff to write the types of questions they are probably best at writing.

- This is the most expensive and most time-consuming option, but may provide the district with the best information about how well students are achieving.

Option B ☐ **Use open-ended questions only for curriculum objectives that cannot be adequately tested with multiple-choice questions.**

- This will be acceptable to many teachers and to all parents.

- This provides a balance of questions in district tests that both teachers and students might find appealing.

- This requires the district to spend additional time in test administration and additional money in scoring only when it is imperative to do so.

Option C ☐ **Do not use open-ended questions in district tests.**

- This will be acceptable to only some teachers, but to most parents.

- This is the least expensive option.

- This requires the least testing time for students

Issue 15: Test "Forms" and Test Question "Pools"

If you decide to develop and use district tests, you will need to decide right away how those tests will be put together. Will there be one version—called a "form"—of each test that is kept locked away in the central office and pulled out every May? Will there be multiple forms of each test that are given in different years in order to keep the test relatively secure? Or will there be a pool of test questions from which questions can be pulled at random whenever a different form of the test is needed?

There are many factors that must be weighed relative to one another when making this decision, including cost of development, feasibility of administration and scoring, security of the tests themselves, and comparability of the results. Here are a couple of our experiences.

We once produced a reading testing program for grades 1–9 for a large Midwestern city by convening more than 100 district teachers and reading supervisors and presiding over the creation of an enormous pool of test questions in which each individual reading objective could be tested by a group of 10 to 20 different multiple-choice test questions. (We will never forget the seventh grade teachers, who drafted 18 test questions on *fore-shadowing*. Unfortunately, none of them were about foreshadowing. They all had to be rewritten. That makes the case for editing by experts, but that is another story.) The final pool of edited test questions let the district create many different forms of each test without ever repeating the exact same set of questions.

While it seems understandable that we could do that in a large city with many teachers and central office specialists as well as the resources of a nearby state university, we actually did something quite similar in a tiny rural district in northern California. Its test question pools—matched, of course, to the district's objectives in each grade and subject—were written by the district's own teachers, edited by our staff, and put into computer software, which allowed a school secretary to create tests on demand. Teachers went to the secretary at designated times, told her the objectives that they had covered, and received a computer-generated test that measured those objectives by drawing questions at random out of the district's pool. We did that 15 years ago when computer software was far less capable than today's. New computers and new software now make the use of a pool of test questions much more feasible that it once was.

But the creation of a deep pool of test questions is still a financial concern as well as a technical concern. While a pool may seem like the right solution, it will be expensive and it requires teachers who can write and editors who can critique.

Here are your options:

Option A ☐ **Have one carefully constructed form of each test.**

- This is the least expensive option.

- It provides the best chance that students' scores over several years can be compared fairly so that the board can judge whether student achievement is improving.

- It requires the least effort to administer and score the tests since the same ones are always used (for example, copies of the tests themselves can be kept and re-used from year to year).

- It would be reasonably acceptable to teachers and would be quite acceptable to parents as well.

Option B ☐ **Have two equivalent forms of each test and give them in alternate years.**

- This is more expensive that one form, but not nearly as expensive as having a pool of test questions.

- It allows for better test security because the same test is not being given every year, thus making it less tempting for teachers to teach exactly what will be on the test and for students to pass answers along to their younger friends.

- It requires relatively little effort to administer and score alternate forms of a test since there are only two to be dealt with.

- It would be reasonably acceptable to teachers and would be quite acceptable to parents as well.

Option C ☐ **Have a pool of test questions for every objective that is to be tested.**

- The process of creating a deep pool can give classroom teachers a clearer understanding of what they want students to learn.

- It enables the district to distribute one or more randomly constructed test forms to teachers for optional use with their own classes during the year.

- This provides the best test security because no one knows until the last minute what questions will be on the test, regardless of whether those tests are called for by teachers individually for their own classes or by the central office for the whole district.

- This would be least acceptable to teachers, but would be quite acceptable to parents.

Issue 16: Board Inspection of Actual Tests

If you call for tests to be created and used districtwide, should board members inspect those actual tests? Can you learn anything by doing that?

Inasmuch as district tests would be based on the district's curriculum, which would have been studied and adopted by the board, it could be argued that the board would not need to see the actual tests. But there may be other things you want to know. The most typical question we have heard is this: How hard are the test questions? Board members understand that a test can be made hard or easy, irrespective of the curriculum objectives that are being assessed. And there has been a lot of press about some states' high school graduation tests being written at a middle school level. That could make board members worry about their own district tests.

We worked for a particularly demanding, yet insightful, board in the Northeast for a couple of years. The board had called for districtwide tests in English across the elementary and middle school grades. They were to be based on a new set of curriculum objectives we had prepared with their teachers during the previous year. We had written the test questions and had gotten them reviewed and approved by committees of teachers. We told the board members that the tests would be interesting for students and demanding as well. We vouched for the tests as outside experts, whom the board had recently trusted with a variety of important curriculum projects. We said everything that we could in favor of the tests, but we finally decided that the board members needed to see the actual questions. We got the administrators to agree—on a split decision.

One thing we had done made that decision easier to make and to execute. We had written two forms of the tests and had planned to use them in alternate years until more could be developed. But there was so much concern from the teachers who were not part of the test review committees—who were, not surprisingly, quite wary of the new district tests—that we decided it would be politic to give away one form to teachers to use in their classes as they wished during the school year. It was then an easy step to decide to give that same form in each grade to board members as well. The board members turned out to be remarkably good at judging both the quality and the difficulty of the test questions. But that did not really surprise us. They had been just as good at judging the curriculum objectives earlier. As soon as the board members had a chance to read through some of the tests, they were satisfied, knowing what was being expected of the students.

Would it work so well with all boards? Our guess is that it may not. Do all boards want that degree of involvement? Our guess is that many do not. What is the right degree of involvement for your board? Here are your options:

Option A ☐ Do not inspect actual test questions.

- This choice supports the idea that the staff can explain what the tests are like to the board sufficiently for the board to be satisfied.

- This is the choice that most administrators would prefer.

- It accepts the notion that many board members would not be comfortable inspecting actual test questions and would feel that they were not qualified to do so.

50

Option B ☐ **Inspect a sample of actual test questions—in an alternate form or drawn randomly from a pool—prior to test administration.**

- This choice allows the board to see the kinds of questions that will be asked and, thus, to discuss with the staff whether the questions seem appropriate.

- It gives the board the background it needs to answer any criticism from teachers about the testing program.

- It prepares the board to answer any complaints from students and their parents about the testing program.

Option C ☐ **Inspect the actual tests prior to test administration.**

- This choice equips the board to ask the staff for explanations or for revisions if the questions in the actual tests seem too hard or too easy or inappropriate in some other way.

- It gives the board the background it needs to answer any criticism from teachers about the tests themselves.

- It prepares the board to answer any complaints from students and their parents about the tests themselves.

Option D ☐ **Inspect actual tests after test administration.**

- This choice sends the actual tests to the board along with the test scores, thus showing the board what the scores represent at the moment the board is examining those scores.

- It prevents any concern about test security caused by board members' having seen the tests before they were administered.

- It will be more comfortable for most administrators to show tests to the board after the fact.

Issue 17: Frequency of Measurement

The administration of nationally standardized tests occurs typically once a year. Sometimes the district has a choice of giving such tests in the fall or in the spring. But it is still a once-a-year event.

State tests are administered on a schedule chosen by state officials. State tests, too, are typically given once a year—in the fall in some states and in the spring in other states. But, in either case, the decision is not yours.

However, when it comes to any district tests that you are developing and administering, the choice of how often to give them is, in fact, yours. As you will see, there are powerful arguments for frequent testing and powerful arguments against it.

We once worked in a Southern city where we had helped to write and implement new curricula across the elementary grades in language arts, mathematics, science, social studies, and health. The superintendent worried that teachers would have trouble keeping up after such a radical change. He also worried that students would fall behind and that no one would know until it was too late for them to catch up. Therefore, he decided to give district tests at the end of every marking period, which was every six weeks. It was an enormous amount of work for his central office administrators and subject specialists—and it had an enormous payoff in student learning in just one year.

But here is the opposite approach. Some years earlier, we had undertaken a complete curriculum overhaul in a district up on the border with Canada—all subjects K–12 in one school year. It was wildly ambitious, but oddly successful. District tests were written by teachers, under our supervision, during the following two years. District administrators decided to give them as final exams at the end of the school year, arguing that anything the students couldn't remember until then hadn't been learned sufficiently well. That was a persuasive argument, we thought at the time. The board wholeheartedly agreed.

How can two opposite approaches both be so reasonable? If you have district tests, what will you do? Here are your options:

Option A ☐ **Give district tests at the end of the school year.**

- This schedule minimizes the cost, time, and intrusiveness of testing.

- This schedule produces the best evidence not only of what students have learned, but also of what they have remembered.

- This schedule gives teachers the best opportunity to demonstrate what they can accomplish in a full year—though they will worry that students will forget things they knew perfectly well earlier in the year.

Option B ☐ **Give district tests at the ends of the semesters.**

- This schedule gives the board and other audiences two chances to judge student achievement during the year.

- The superintendent, other administrators, and teachers have the chance to correct any shortcomings of the first semester during the second semester.

- Students do not have to remember the entire first semester's learning throughout the second semester in order to demonstrate it on an end-of-year test.

- Two semester tests can cover more material than one end-of-year test, without being too long for students to take.

Option C ☐ **Give district tests at the ends of the marking periods.**

- This schedule gives the board and other audiences several chances to judge student achievement during the year.

- Principals and teachers can monitor student learning closely and can intervene when necessary to make improvements before future learning is compromised.

- District tests that have been carefully developed can be used by teachers to replace (or supplement) their own marking-period tests.

- Several marking-period tests can cover even more material than two end-of-semester tests, still without being too long for students to take.

Option D ☐ **Give district tests at the ends of instructional units.**

- This schedule gives the board and other audiences many chances to judge student achievement during the year.

- This schedule gives students their best chance at doing well because it allows the least amount of time for forgetting.

- Teachers can get early and repeated evidence as to what students are—or are not—learning and can shape their teaching during the remainder of the year accordingly.

- Multiple instructional-unit tests can cover more material than several end-of-marking-period tests, still without being too long for students to take.

Option E ☐ **Give district tests on whatever schedule you choose.**

- Rather than fixing the evaluation searchlight on selected targets at scheduled times, this allows the board to swivel it to illuminate any aspect of student learning at any time.

- Single snapshots of diverse aspects of student learning at various grades can be more informative than a multi-year series of snapshots of the same subject and grade over and over again.

- Uncertainty about which aspects of student learning will be evaluated when will make teachers more likely to teach all of the district's required curriculum objectives.

Issue 18: Sampling Students

Districts should probably make more use of sampling in creating testing programs than they do—both for nationally standardized tests and for local district tests. Sampling can yield considerable savings in testing time for students and for teachers as well as in expense for the district.

Admittedly, students not included in a sample cannot benefit directly from the tests, but they can benefit indirectly from any program improvements arising from the findings for the sample—and that might be enough. Indeed, we like to think of district tests as testing the curriculum rather than testing the students. That is, the question being answered is whether sixth grade English is working, not whether Alvin is working. For the former, you don't need every student to participate. As for Alvin, you presumably are not interested in his individual test score—we would argue that you as a board should not be—so you can leave him out at random and still learn all you need to know about sixth grade English.

If you still need to relax more about sampling, here is the most important thing to remember: *A test is just a sample of behavior.* In other words, no single test can tell you everything a student—or a room full of students, or a school full of students, or a district full of students—knows about a subject. Any single test simply asks students about some aspects of what they have been learning. No test can ask questions about all possible aspects of what they have been learning. Therefore, the concept of sampling is built fundamentally into the world of testing.

To shorten the discussion, let's assume, for openers, that you will not test all grades and all subjects every year, even if you decide to have an extensive district testing program. That amount of testing would be overwhelming for everyone concerned. You will sample grades and subjects—albeit, hopefully, a generous and well-selected sample.

But even within the grades and subjects you choose, you will not test all of your curriculum objectives. First, they are too numerous. Second, some of them do not lend themselves to speedy enough, cheap enough, or valid enough testing (we are thinking especially of curriculum objectives that describe students' attitudes). Thus, we will assume at the outset that you will test only a sample of your district's curriculum objectives every year—albeit, hopefully, a generous and well-selected sample.

On the other hand, let's also assume that you will *not* sample schools (if you are in a large district with, for example, a number of elementary schools). You will presumably decide that at least some classrooms in each school should be tested so that no segment of the district's population is left out. Whether you as board members should look at the results for individual schools separately is another question that is worth its own chapter. But, for now, let us move forward under the presumption that you will have tests given to at least some students in each of your schools.

That brings us to classrooms. Logistically, it would be quite inconvenient to test some students in a classroom or a section (in the middle and high school grades) and not test others. What would the teacher do with the untested? So, presumably having decided to sample subjects and grades and objectives, do you now sample classrooms/sections?

Here are your two options:

Option A ☐ **Sample classrooms/sections.**

- This yields the same board-level information about student achievement that would have come from testing all students.

- It reduces testing costs.

- It reduces administrative time and effort in setting up and running large-scale districtwide testing programs.

- It allows the district to use the savings to extend the testing program to cover other grades and/or subjects, thus yielding more board-level information in additional areas.

- It reduces testing time and test anxiety for students not tested.

Option B ☐ **Do not sample classrooms/sections.**

- This avoids any controversy about the adequacy of the method of sampling and, thus, about whether the test results accurately represent all students.

- It makes it possible to calculate trends in test results from year to year without having to consider "sampling error."

- It enables every teacher to use the test results to improve the teaching of every student (if the test results come back early enough).

- It enables every teacher to use the test results from a carefully developed district test to give every student a grade—perhaps equivalent to a final exam grade.

- It makes it possible to inform every parent of the achievement of his or her own child.

Issue 19: Setting Standards

You cannot judge test scores without a standard—a standard declaring how high the scores should be. Otherwise, looking at test scores is a meaningless waste of time, equivalent to reading pressure gauges without knowing what the pressures should be. Test scores cannot announce that they are low or high. You have to judge them against a standard you yourselves have established as a board. This is true whether you are looking at nationally standardized tests, state tests, or your own district tests.

The best case we ever saw of standard setting came from a Southern city where we had been working closely with an aggressive superintendent on improving the district's nationally standardized test scores. In the first week of school, he called his 40 principals together. He handed out graphs of their scores from the previous spring and asked them to draw new lines onto the graphs—new lines that would represent the scores their students would get the following spring. The principals resisted. How could they make such promises? Could they have more time? Could they meet with their teachers first? The superintendent was unrelenting. At the end of the session, the principals turned in what came to be known as their "promise lines." The act of promising—of setting standards—had a powerful impact. When the superintendent averaged out the promise lines across the schools, he promised the board that the district would go up 5 national percentile points that year. Everyone worked hard, mindful of their promises. The district went up 10 national percentile points in that one year. Setting standards helped make that happen.

Remember that there are two different kinds of standards: *absolute* and *comparative*. An absolute standard is a desired point on a scale—a scale independent of anyone's actual performance. It is chosen as a criterion for judging a district's performance—irrespective of what other districts do. In contrast, a comparative standard is also a desired point—but this time a scale that is literally created by the actual performances of others. While an absolute standard neither knows nor cares what other districts do, a comparative standard knows and cares about nothing except what other districts do.

Scores on nationally standardized tests are usually reported as comparative scores (often percentiles or stanines). In all such cases, you have no choice: You must adopt a comparative standard. For example, a board might say, "The district shall score at or above the 60th national percentile. . . ." Such a standard, though it sounds absolute, will actually fluctuate over time according to what students in other districts do on the test.

Scores on state tests are often expressed in absolute terms—for example, the percent of students scoring at given levels, such as *basic* or *proficient*. In such cases, you can adopt either an absolute standard or a comparative standard. For example, a board could express an absolute standard in these terms: "95 percent of our district's students in grade 5 shall score at the *basic* level or above on the State's mathematics test." Or it could choose to adopt a comparative standard, such as this: "The district's average score on the State's mathematics test in grade 5 shall be at or above the average for all districts in our socioeconomic category."

Scores on any district tests you give will have to be judged against an absolute standard since no out-of-district students take those tests. Inasmuch as district tests would be based squarely on the curriculum adopted by the board, the absolute standard would express how well you expect that curriculum to be learned. It follows that the board's standard is likely to be reasonably high—for example, "80 percent of students in grade 8 will achieve a passing score of 70 or better on the district's science test."

You can adopt standards for any or all of the tests used in the district testing program. [Note: We exclude from this discussion the standards for tests created and scored by individual teachers, for which the each teacher will set his or her own absolute standards (the teacher's own ideas of good and bad scores) or comparative standards (grading "on the curve").]

Here are your options (you can, of course, select a combination of options or different options for different grades and/or subjects):

Option A ☐ **Set standards for any nationally standardized tests given in the district.**

- This is the only way the board can express to district administrators and teachers how well it wants the students to score compared to other students nationwide.

- It is the only way the board can notify parents and taxpayers how well district students measure up to the board's standards on national yardsticks.

- This is comfortable for both educators and the public because of the use of nationally standardized tests over many years.

Option B ☐ **Set standards for any required and/or optional state tests given in the district.**

- This is the only way the board can express to district administrators and teachers how well it wants the students to score on the state's goals.

- It is the only way the board can notify parents and taxpayers how well district students measure up to the board's standards on state yardsticks.

- This is not so comfortable for either educators or the public in many states yet, but will probably become increasingly so as state tests become more visible over the next decade.

Option C ☐ **Set standards for any local tests created and given in the district.**

- This is the only way the board can express to district administrators and teachers how well it wants the students to learn the particular curriculum goals and objectives established by the board for them.

- It is the only way the board can notify parents and taxpayers how well district students are meeting the board's standards on what it set forth for them to learn.

- This is not so comfortable for either educators or the public in most school districts yet, but will probably become increasingly so if district tests continue to become more common over the next decade.

Issue 20: Analyses, Interpretations, and Recommendations Accompanying Test Results

We often wonder what board members are thinking when they get reports of test results at a board meeting from the testing director or another administrator. We have heard many, many such presentations—of results from nationally standardized tests, state tests, and district tests—and too often we ourselves cannot understand them. And we do this for a living. As we frequently say to each other after such occasions, "That person was trying to explain away the results, not explain them." To hear many of these individuals tell it, the test results mean very little—for a myriad of reasons, which get discussed more than the actual results.

Now, of course, sometimes things happen that need to be discussed. Sometimes a state will write a brand new physics test for high school students that most of the students in the state—even at highly selective honors high schools—fail. When that happens, board members do have to understand the context of the test scores and that the students' scores are probably not reflective of their actual learning. But that is not usually the case. And board members need to understand that as well.

In 1982, we hosted a session at the American Educational Research Association annual meeting called "Plain Talk." It was designed to show researchers and school district testing directors how to talk to board members: plainly, calmly, and jargon-free. We had excellent models at that session, including the brilliant and amazingly approachable Robert L. Ebel, of Michigan State University, who could explain the most complicated concept to a lay audience in the most common sense way. At that session, Professor Ebel, who died later that year, answered this question: "Are we putting a loaded gun in the hands of a baby when we give lay school board members comprehensive, sophisticated student test results with which to judge the success of the professional educators who work for them?" He said this:

No. We're giving groups of mature men and women who are ethically and intellectually superior to most of the rest of us access to information that can contribute greatly to the effective management of the enterprise for which they are responsible and in which we all have such a major interest. Let me try to justify such a strong statement, such an unqualified assertion. Many of us are too heavily committed to our own purposes, our own interests and concerns, to donate substantial amounts of our time and energy to public service on a board of education. . . . We have too little concern for what Walter Lippmann called "the public philosophy." Most men and women who become candidates for school board membership do so from a genuine concern for the public good of the local community. Some may have an ax to grind, but they quickly discover that there is far more demanded of them than grinding that particular ax. By and large, members of local school boards are less selfish, more public spirited than the rest of us. In that respect, they are ethically superior. To campaign successfully for election to a school board requires intelligence as well as commitment and energy. One must make statements and answer questions intelligently. One must be well informed about the purposes and problems of the local schools. One who displays ignorance in any of these areas of relevant knowledge is unlikely to be elected by one's fellow citizens to board membership. It is in this respect that they are likely to be intellectually superior to most of the rest of us.

It is common for boards to receive test results without analyses, such as breakdowns by race; without interpretations as to why the results have changed or not changed since last time; and without recommendations as to how board policy or administrative practice should be modified to increase learning. The absence of such administrative commentary limits the value of having a testing program and reduces the board's ability to initiate improvements in student achievement. Let's remember what Professor Ebel thought of you. Raise the bar. Ask for what you need in order to make the best use of the results.

Here are the board's options for increasing the utility of the testing program (you could choose a combination of these options, if they appeal to you):

Option A ☐ Require analyses of test results.

- This will stimulate the staff to display scores by any categories that the board has stipulated and any other categories that add meaning to the data.

- It will stimulate the staff to look within the results for evidence of differential learning among the several strands of content and skills that were tested in a particular subject field, such as numeration, computation, and problem-solving in mathematics

- It will stimulate the staff to display trends over time.

Option B ☐ Require interpretation of test results.

- This will stimulate the staff to correlate test scores with student activities presumed to affect learning in order to judge their effect, such as using computers, doing homework, and participating in community internships.

- It will stimulate the staff to identify events in preceding years that may have influenced any trend in the results.

- It will lead the staff to identify recent program changes that were predicted to improve learning and reach conclusions about their actual effect.

Option C ☐ Require data-based recommendations as to how learning can be improved.

- This will remind the staff that a major purpose of testing—and its greatest value—is to improve learning.

- It will stimulate the staff to go through its analyses and interpretations seeking influences on test scores that could be changed by future shifts in board policy and/or administrative practice.

- It will cause the staff to formulate recommendations in the context of test results, knowing that the board has tools for evaluating whether and how those recommendations—if adopted—actually improve learning.

Sample Documents for Board Members

Sample Board Policy—The Board's Role in the Curriculum Development Process

Sample Board Policy—Social Studies (in the Elementary Schools)

Sample Board Policy—Foreign Languages (in the High Schools)

Sample Board Policy—Curriculum Objectives

Sample Explanation of Curriculum Objectives (*for giving to teachers, administrators, and board members along with new curriculum objectives*)

Sample Parent Checklist Front Cover (*for sending curriculum objectives home to parents*)

Sample Parent Checklist Back Cover (*for sending curriculum objectives home to parents*)

Sample Curriculum Objectives
Grade 2 Art

Sample Board Policy

The Board's Role in the Curriculum Development Process

The Board's Role in the Curriculum Development Cycle

Advance Guidance by the Board. The Board shall provide guidance to the Superintendent about each subject field immediately in advance of the beginning of the curriculum development cycle for that subject. The Board shall indicate its position on subject-specific significant issues of curriculum content, such as the emphases to be given to various components of that subject in the elementary, middle, and/or high schools.

Review by the Board of Research Findings. After the committee of District staff has completed the initial research stage of the curriculum development cycle in each subject field—that is, after all outside sources and District sources of potential curriculum content have been investigated and after all background data have been analyzed—the Superintendent shall submit the findings of the committee to the Board for review.

The Board's reactions shall be used to guide the second stage of the curriculum development cycle—that is, the writing of K–12 outcomes, of benchmarks for clusters of grades, and of specific grade-by-grade elementary and middle school indicators and specific middle and high school course indicators.

Review and Adoption by the Board of Outcomes, Benchmarks, and Indicators. The Superintendent shall submit the proposed outcomes, benchmarks, and indicators in each subject field to the Board for review, possible modification, and approval and adoption as the District's official curriculum.

The Board's Role in the Curriculum Development Process Off Cycle

The Board may provide direction at any time to the Superintendent on significant issues of community concern related to the curriculum content in any subject field. Based on such direction, the Superintendent shall have the outcomes, benchmarks, and/or grade-by-grade and course objectives in that subject field revised by District staff within a reasonably short period of time and shall present the revised version to the Board for approval and adoption.

This policy was written in cooperation with the administrators and board members of the Blue Valley Schools (Overland Park, Kansas) and was adopted by the Blue Valley board in June, 2000.

Sample Board Policy

Social Studies (in the Elementary Schools)

The social studies curriculum in the elementary schools shall provide a balance of knowledge, skills, and attitudes in the social studies disciplines of history, geography, civics and government, economics, and sociology and culture in each grade K–5, with an emphasis on history, geography, and civics and government.

Critical thinking, problem-solving, decision-making, communications, and research skills as applied to social studies content shall be taught in each grade.

While the focus in the earlier grades may be on the student's family and community, appropriate content from the important disciplines of history, geography, and civics and government shall be included even in those grades. While the focus in the later grades may be on cities and regions of the U.S. as well as on the early history of our country from exploration through the Constitution, appropriate content from selected social studies disciplines about selected significant countries across all other continents shall also be taught in a systematic fashion so that introductory information about all continents is provided by the end of grade 5.

The grade-level indicators written for the social studies curriculum in each grade K–5 shall meet or exceed all social studies standards established by the state of Kansas as well as all applicable social studies standards published by nationally recognized curriculum advisory commissions in the various social studies disciplines, including history, geography, civics, and economics.

History

While a formal study of history shall begin with early U.S. history in grade 5, students in grades K–4 shall learn historical information about their local community, the state of Kansas, and the U.S, using methods and materials appropriate for young students, including biographies of famous individuals and stories of famous historical events.

Students shall understand the customs, traditions, and stories of various peoples in the early history of the U.S.

Students shall develop a sense of chronological time, describe cause–effect relationships between significant events, and understand how and why accounts of events may differ. They shall understand the historical roots of national holidays and selected current events. They shall explain the impact of inventions and technology over time.

Geography

Students shall name and locate the continents and major oceans and seas of the world on a world map. They shall also name major physical geographic features of all of the continents, including rivers and mountains.

Students shall name important physical geographic features of their local community, the state of Kansas, and the U.S., including rivers, lakes, and mountains (e.g., the Mississippi River, the Great Lakes, the Rocky Mountains). They shall also describe the physical boundaries and the climate regions of the U.S. Students shall locate the 50 states on a map of the U.S. and shall name the capitals of the states and other major cities of the U.S.

Students shall describe the impact of physical features on people and the impact of people on the environment, both historically and today.

Students shall define and use geographic terminology appropriately. They shall create and use various types of maps effectively in appropriate situations, including the use of scales, latitude and longitude, and cardinal and intermediate directions.

Civics and Government

Students shall understand the need for laws and shall respect the rights and responsibilities of citizenship. They shall have a basic understanding of and appreciation for important documents in our history, especially the Declaration of Independence and the Constitution.

Students shall describe the functions and structure of their local government, the Kansas state government, and the U.S. government, and they shall name their current leaders. They shall understand our system of elections and shall appreciate the importance of participating, becoming informed, and performing public service.

Economics

Students shall have a basic understanding of fundamental economic concepts, including public and private goods and services; producers and consumers; forms of exchange; supply and demand; price and cost, including opportunity cost; scarcity; competition; and natural, human, and capital resources.

Students shall understand the importance of making wise choices when spending and saving money.

Students shall recognize the importance of trade among states and among nations and shall see how states and nations are economically interdependent.

Students shall describe how goods are manufactured and distributed, including the role of assembly lines, specialization of labor, and technology. They shall name important industries and products, both manufactured and agricultural, of Kansas and of various regions of the U.S.

Sociology and Culture

Students shall describe and appreciate historical and contemporary cultural influences on their lives.

Students shall respect the customs and traditions of peoples around the world and within the U.S. They shall compare and contrast their own traditions with other traditions, past and present. They shall describe the contributions of various peoples to the history of the U.S. and to contemporary society.

Students shall describe the components of culture and the importance of each to society. Students shall describe past and present cultures and lifestyles in the U.S.

Students shall use the concepts of race, gender, and class to describe historical and contemporary individuals and groups.

This policy was written in cooperation with the administrators and board members of the Blue Valley Schools (Overland Park, Kansas) and was adopted by the Blue Valley board in June, 2000.

Sample Board Policy

Foreign Languages (in the High Schools)

Each high school shall provide foreign language instruction for students through elective courses in modern and classical foreign languages—French, German, Spanish, and Latin. When economically and logistically feasible, additional modern foreign languages representing important countries or regions of the world shall be added.

Appropriate levels of each language shall be provided in each high school for students beginning a new language or continuing with their elementary and/or middle school language—at least levels I, II, III, and IV, though not necessarily in separate course sections. When economically and logistically feasible, Advanced Placement courses shall be provided in each of the modern and classical languages offered in each school.

Students continuing with their elementary and/or middle school language shall be expected to place into level II or III courses when they enter high school and shall be so placed, based on the recommendation of their grade 8 foreign language teacher, their past foreign language grades, and their demonstrated foreign language skills.

In the high school courses, the modern foreign language curriculum shall provide a balance of knowledge, skills, and attitudes in reading, writing, speaking, listening, and culture. The classical foreign language curriculum shall provide a balance of knowledge, skills, and attitudes primarily in reading and culture.

In the high school courses in the modern foreign languages, teachers shall provide instruction in the foreign language being studied rather than in English.

The course indicators written for each course in the high school foreign language curriculum shall meet or exceed all foreign language standards established by the state of Kansas as well as all applicable foreign language standards published by nationally recognized foreign language curriculum advisory commissions.

Reading

Students in lower-level modern foreign language courses shall read stories, poems, and informational texts as well as authentic documents in the language, including, but not limited to, newspapers and magazines. Students in upper-level modern foreign language courses shall read informational texts, a wider variety of authentic documents, and recognized literature in the language—including, but not limited to, novels, poems, and plays—of appropriate difficulty and content.

Students in classical foreign language courses shall translate recognized literature in the language—including both poetry and various types of prose, such as histories and essays—of appropriate difficulty and content.

Students in lower-level classical foreign language courses shall have facility with all noun declensions; with verb conjugations in a limited number of present, past, and future tenses; and with the construction of simple, compound, and complex sentences with multiple prepositional phrases. Students in upper-level classical foreign language courses shall also have facility with verb conjugations in all tenses and moods and with the construction of increasingly complex sentences.

Culture

Students in all modern foreign language courses shall learn about the cultures of selected countries and regions that speak the language, including an examination of the past and present effects of those cultures on our own American culture (e.g., food, dress, music, art, literature, borrowed words). Students shall investigate the everyday life of the people—including their customs, food, dress, holidays, housing, transportation, education, and family structure—as described in authentic documents or by authentic sources (such as native speakers) when possible. Students shall study geographic features, cities, and landmarks as well as important historical events and well-known past and present individuals in these countries and regions.

Students in all classical foreign language courses shall learn about the cultures of the countries and regions of the world that once spoke the language, including an examination of the present effects of those long-ago cultures on our own American culture (e.g., art, literature, government, religion). The effects of the classical language on English as well as on other modern foreign languages shall also be analyzed. Students shall investigate the everyday life of the people living in those ancient times, including their customs, food, dress, holidays, housing, transportation, education, and family structure. Students shall study geographic features and well-known cities as well as important historical events and well-known historical figures in those cultures.

Writing

Students in lower-level modern foreign language courses shall communicate in writing using a variety of declarative, interrogatory, exclamatory, and imperative sentences. They shall also write a variety of descriptive, narrative, and expository paragraphs. Students in upper-level modern foreign language courses shall also write longer texts for personal use (e.g., letters) and for school (e.g., brief informational reports, literary criticism).

Students in lower-level modern foreign language courses shall be expected to use correct grammar and usage when writing, including, but not limited to, correct spelling; proper sentence construction; correct verb forms in a limited number of present, past, and future tenses; use of pronouns; and agreement of nouns and adjectives. Students in upper-level modern foreign language courses shall also be expected to write correctly using a wider vocabulary, an increased number of verb tenses and moods, and more complex sentence constructions.

Speaking

Students in all modern foreign language courses shall speak in the language in whole-class as well as in small-group settings. Teachers shall emphasize students' ability to speak with a native accent and correct pronunciation of words. Students shall be expected to use a wider vocabulary as well as to construct simple declarative, interrogatory, exclamatory, and imperative sentences. In addition, in upper-level modern foreign language courses, students shall speak to the whole class or larger groups of students when making various types of presentations (e.g., when presenting a report, when reading or reciting a poem aloud).

Students in lower-level modern foreign language courses shall be expected to use reasonably correct grammar and usage when speaking, including, but not limited to, proper sentence construction; correct verb forms in a limited number of present, past, and future tenses; and agreement of nouns and adjectives.

Students in upper-level modern foreign language courses shall be expected to use reasonably correct grammar and usage when speaking, including, but not limited to, complex sentence construction and correct verb forms in all tenses and moods. They shall be expected to communicate reasonably clearly in an everyday conversation with native speakers.

Listening

Students in all modern foreign language courses shall listen to the language in whole-class as well as in small-group settings, with the teacher and other students as the speakers as well as with others from outside the classroom as the speakers. Students shall also listen to native speakers in person or through technological means.

Students in all modern foreign language courses shall be able to comprehend the main ideas and most details of what they hear in the language.

This policy was written in cooperation with the administrators and board members of the Blue Valley Schools (Overland Park, Kansas) and was adopted by the Blue Valley board in June, 2000.

Sample Board Policy

Curriculum Objectives

An orderly series of curriculum objectives that describe student learning shall be adopted by the Board of Education in each subject for each grade or course.

Characteristics of Individual Objectives

Each individual objective shall have the following characteristics:

1. Fit the goals of the community.

2. Be important for students to learn. That is, each objective shall be important either in and of itself or as a foundation supporting some important, more advanced objective.

3. Describe something that can successfully be taught to at least 80 percent of the students during the regular school day, given their intellectual maturity and social experience at their age.

4. Describe the student learning intended as a result of finishing the grade or the course: (1) factual knowledge or an intellectual skill (the cognitive domain); (2) an attitude, feeling, or belief (the affective domain); or (3) a muscular skill involving body movement, including sensory skills involving one of the five senses (the psychomotor domain).

5. Be classifiable into specific levels—from basic to advanced—in each of the three domains (e.g., Benjamin Bloom's taxonomy for the cognitive domain).

6. Be specific and detailed.

7. Be measurable by valid and reliable objective or subjective methods.

8. Be simply and clearly worded so that most lay people can read and understand it.

Characteristics of the Set of Objectives for Each Grade or Course

The set of objectives adopted in each subject for each grade or course shall have the following characteristics:

1. Be at a level of difficulty that challenges hard-working students.

2. Cover a coherent and comprehensive set of topics within the subject for that grade or course.

3. Cover the cognitive and affective domains of learning.

4. Cover the psychomotor domain of leaning as appropriate for the subject at that grade or in that course.

5. Have a reasonable share of the objectives in the upper, more advanced levels of the cognitive, affective, and/or psychomotor domains, as appropriate for the subject at that grade or in that course.

6. Be more difficult than the set of objectives adopted for the preceding grade or course in that subject and have no overlap of objectives from the preceding grade or course. That is, each objective shall appear in only one grade or course (except for remedial courses, in which all of the objectives have appeared in an earlier grade or course).

7. Be scheduled to be taught in marking periods (e.g., quarters, semesters) and be assigned to marking periods according to a logical teaching sequence.

Sources of Objectives

Several of the following sources shall be used in seeking ideas for objectives or in seeking actual objectives to be adapted or adopted without change:

1. District faculty members in the appropriate subjects, grades, and courses.

2. District administrators.

3. District Board of Education members.

4. Textbooks and related instructional materials in the subject at the appropriate grade or for the appropriate course.

5. Outside examinations, such as those published by commercial testing companies or those issued by state or federal government agencies.

6. Nationally recognized experts in the subject field.

7. Nationally recognized experts in the preparation of objectives.

8. Other school districts.

9. Associations of professional educators in specific subjects (e.g., the American Council on the Teaching of Foreign Languages).

10. Curriculum publications of the state education department.

Brief documentation concerning the use of these sources, along with any others deemed appropriate by district faculty members and administrators, shall be made by the professional staff. That documentation shall be reviewed by the Board of Education prior to the adoption of objectives for any grade or course.

Review of Objectives

Before the objectives for any grade or course are recommended to the Board of Education for adoption, they shall be reviewed and critiqued by individuals from several of the following categories, working independently of each other:

1. District faculty members in the appropriate subjects, grades, or courses.

2. District administrators.

3. Nationally recognized experts in the subject field.

4. Nationally recognized experts in the preparation of objectives.

5. Professors in the subject field.

6. Faculty members in other school districts.

7. Employers in occupational fields related to the subject field (especially as reviewers for vocational education courses).

Reviewers shall be supplied with specific criteria for objectives, as outlined in this policy, as the basis for their critiques.

Brief documentation shall be made by the professional staff of the critiques provided by the reviewers. The documentation shall be reviewed by the Board of Education prior to the adoption of objectives for any grade or course.

The professional staff shall review all adopted objectives for all grades and courses at least annually and shall recommend to the Board of Education any changes that may be warranted. Depending on the magnitude of any changes, the Board of Education may seek outside reviews and critiques before adopting or rejecting the changes recommended.

Uses of Objectives

After the objectives for any grade or course have been adopted by the Board of Education, they shall be used for the following purposes, among others:

1. Selecting textbooks and other instructional materials for the grade or course.

2. Acquainting newly employed district teachers with the objectives for the grade or courses they will be teaching.

3. Training current district teachers, if necessary, in any revised subject matter content and/or in instructional methods for teaching that content.

4. Informing parents as to what their children are expected to learn in each grade or course.

5. Selecting and/or creating objective and/or subjective tests to see whether the objectives for each grade and course have been met.

Brief documentation of each of these uses shall be made by the professional staff. That documentation shall be reviewed by the Board of Education regularly.

> *This policy was written originally in cooperation with the administrators and board members of Township High School District 211 (Palatine, Illinois), was adopted by that board in 1984, and has since been used as a model for many other school districts across the U.S.*

Sample Explanation of Curriculum Objectives

> ## Some Explanatory Notes for the Greenwich Curriculum Objectives in Reading/Language Arts K–8
>
> *November, 2001*

Here is an explanation of the conventions used in the Greenwich reading/language arts objectives for grades K–8:

1. **Mastery of the objectives**

   Each objective is placed in the grade at which mastery is expected by about 80 percent of Greenwich students by the end of the school year. It is expected that teachers will make every effort to help the remaining 20 percent of Greenwich students also achieve mastery and that the district will provide additional resources to the degree possible to assist in that effort.

   In some grades in some strands of the curriculum (such as in the punctuation, capitalization, and grammar strand), these objectives represent an elaboration and expansion of the district's current curriculum. Therefore, 80 percent of Greenwich students may not achieve mastery of these objectives for several years.

2. **Continuous progress**

   It is clear to all Greenwich teachers that continuous progress is our goal for students and that students should move ahead with the objectives as they are able. To that end, teachers will need to look forward to the objectives in a later grade to challenge some students in their classes, just as they will need to look back at the objectives from a previous grade to help improve the skills of other students in their classes. To the degree that this is feasible and beneficial for individual students or small groups of students, teachers are strongly encouraged to do so.

3. **Freedom to go beyond the objectives**

   While each teacher is required to teach all of the objectives scheduled for his or her grade, each teacher is also free to go beyond them to teach additional knowledge and skills that would be beneficial or of interest to a particular class of students.

4. **Freedom to teach the objectives using a variety of instructional materials and methods**

   In some cases, the district may provide instructional materials for teaching the objectives; in other cases, school buildings will choose and provide their own materials. These decisions will be made following further discussions with teachers, building staff, and district staff.

   Nonetheless, each teacher remains free to use whatever instructional methods seem most appropriate to him or her for teaching the objectives.

5. Freedom to match literary analysis objectives to works taught

There are many literary analysis objectives included in the fiction and nonfiction strands of the curriculum. There will also be core reading lists, created by committees of Greenwich teachers, that will specify works in all of the literary genres to be taught in each grade. Furthermore, teachers are free to teach works beyond those specified on the core reading lists.

Because of the variety and number of literary analysis objectives to be covered and literary works to be taught, it is neither feasible nor necessary for teachers to apply each objective to each work. Therefore, each teacher is free to match those objectives to specific works as he or she wishes, as long as each of the objectives is covered at least once during the school year.

6. Teaching sequence

The objectives may be taught in whatever order makes sense to each individual teacher, grade level, and/or school building. Their presentation in this numbered list format is for ease of use, but is not meant to imply a particular teaching sequence.

Each teacher is free to group the objectives into logical units within reading/language arts and/or to link these objectives to those in other subjects as he or she wishes.

7. Coding to Connecticut's Performance Standards

Any objective that is related to Connecticut's Performance Standards is indicated by an asterisk and a number code in parentheses after the objective. The number in the parentheses indicates one of Connecticut's 33 Performance Standards within its four Content Standards, such as 1.9, 2.5, 3.4, or 4.10. The first number is the number of one of the four Content Standards, each of which is broken down into multiple Performance Standards.

In a few cases, objectives so coded are almost verbatim copies of the explanations of the Performance Standards in Connecticut's Curriculum Trace Maps. In most cases, however, the objectives are more specific, detailed versions of the Performance Standards that are articulated from grade to grade.

8. Coding to CMT and CAPT

Any objective that is related to the state tests—the CMT or CAPT—is indicated by this code after the objective: (CMT) or (CAPT). Such coded objectives generally appear in the grade(s) preceding the grade in which the test is given so that teachers can adequately prepare students for the test in advance.

9. Affective objectives

Some objectives are affective rather than cognitive—that is, they are aimed at shaping the attitudes of students. Research shows, for example, that students' attitudes toward the study of science and mathematics are set for life by the time students are in second grade. Therefore, it is clear that some attention to the attitudes of students is warranted, starting in the early years of schooling and indeed continuing through the later years.

These affective objectives start with verbs such as "enjoys," "appreciates," and "believes." Because it is more difficult to evaluate affective objectives, these objectives will not be part of any formal district assessment.

10. Italicized words

Words that are considered part of the essential terminology of reading/language arts are italicized in the grade in which students are first expected to use them in their own speaking and, when reasonable, in their own writing. Such words include grammatical terms (*noun, prepositional phrase, declarative sentence*, etc.), literary elements (*setting, mood*, etc.), figurative language (*simile, personification*, etc.), genres (*fable, myth, narrative poem*, etc.), and so on.

11. **E.g. *vs.* i.e.**

When an objective includes an *e.g.* statement in parentheses, the examples given in parentheses are simply examples (*e.g.* meaning *exempli gratia*, or *for the sake of an example*). Teachers may use such examples or not as they choose when teaching the objective.

However, if an objective includes an *i.e.* statement in parentheses, that statement is to be included in the teaching of the objective because it is a further explanation of the objective (*i.e.* meaning *id est*, or *that is*). Similarly, if an objective includes a list of items after a colon, those items are also to be taught specifically.

The objectives for all grades K–8 will be conveniently available to Greenwich teachers, both electronically and in print form. Thus, teachers will be able to look back or look ahead to find objectives from earlier or later grades that might be helpful in teaching their own students.

Further, Greenwich teachers should keep their own notes on what works and what does not work while they are teaching the objectives each year. The district is committed to keeping these curriculum objectives up to date by reviewing them as needed at the end of each school year and making whatever minor modifications are necessary before beginning a new school year. While this does not take the place of a full-scale review on the curriculum cycle adopted by the Board, it does ensure that the objectives will always be as up to date as possible and, therefore, as useful as possible for teachers.

This explanation was written originally in cooperation with the language arts curriculum specialist for the Greenwich Public Schools (Greenwich, Connecticut); was distributed to Greenwich teachers, principals, and board members with new K–8 reading/language arts curriculum objectives; and has since been used as a model for other school districts.

Sample Parent Checklist Front Cover

Language Arts and Mathematics Checklist GRADE 2

Dear Parent:

We are raising our standards for student learning in language arts and mathematics. We are doing this for two reasons: (1) the State has raised its standards; and (2) our standards should be higher than the State's.

We have set as our goal that **80 percent**—that is, four out of five students—will learn our new language arts and mathematics objectives each year. But this is the first year of our new objectives, and we may not succeed perfectly—especially in the upper grades where we will be working hard to give students some of the background they might have missed. Of course, we understand that the remaining 20 percent of our students might need additional and special services in order to succeed, and we will be working to provide them as well.

This *Language Arts and Mathematics Checklist* tells exactly what we will be teaching your child this year. These objectives will guide the work of our students, our teachers, and our principals. But the school cannot teach these objectives all alone. Your child will need three things from you: your encouragement, your help, and your checking to see that he or she is working hard in school and studying hard at home.

We expect you as a **parent** to . . .

- Review this *Language Arts and Mathematics Checklist* to see what your child should learn this year.
- Ask your child's teacher or principal about any objectives you do not understand.
- Help your child learn these objectives.
- Make sure your child attends school regularly and arrives on time.
- Follow some of the suggestions on the back of this *Language Arts and Mathematics Checklist*.

We expect your **child** to . . .

- Read at home regularly.
- Work hard at school and study hard at home to learn the objectives.
- Ask the teacher when he or she has a question about the objectives.
- Try very hard on all homework, all projects, and all tests.

We expect your child's **teacher** to . . .

- Teach your child the objectives in this *Language Arts and Mathematics Checklist*.
- Choose the best possible methods and materials for teaching the objectives.
- Talk with you about how you can help your child learn these objectives.
- Monitor your child's progress during the year.

We expect your child's **principal** to . . .

- Know what objectives your child should learn this year.
- Be available to talk with you about how important these objectives are for your child.
- Work with your child's teacher to see that these objectives are taught.
- Provide the books and other materials that your child's teacher needs to teach these objectives.

By giving all of us the same target, this *Language Arts and Mathematics Checklist* will help us work together to improve student learning. Please keep it handy and use it during this school year.

Sincerely,

Chairperson, Board of Education

Sample Parent Checklist Back Cover

THINGS YOU AS A PARENT SHOULD DO

☐ 1. Tell your child that you think these language arts and math objectives are important.

☐ 2. Ask your child regularly what language arts and math objectives he or she is learning in school.

☐ 3. Read to your child or have your child read to you or to himself or herself regularly—preferably every day.

☐ 4. Insist that your child schedule a definite homework time in a quiet place for every school day. If your child has no homework, have your child read or watch a television news program with you and discuss it.

☐ 5. Look over all homework papers before your child takes them to school and after he or she brings them home.

☐ 6. Buy several good reference books (such as a dictionary, thesaurus, encyclopedia, atlas, and almanac) and help your child use them often.

☐ 7. Go to the library regularly with your child and discuss the books that both of you have checked out.

☐ 8. Tell your child how you use language arts and math skills in your job.

☐ 9. Ask your child to tell you about his or her favorite author.

☐ 10. Encourage your child to read nonfiction books about math and history and science as well as fiction books.

☐ 11. Show your child how you use math skills at home in cooking, carpentry, budgeting, shopping, planning trips, and other everyday ways.

☐ 12. Help your child research a topic of interest by using the Internet.

☐ 13. Talk with your child about the importance of knowing the addition, subtraction, multiplication, and division math facts by heart.

☐ 14. Talk with your child about the importance of good grammar, spelling, capitalization, and punctuation in the world of work.

☐ 15. Help your child apply measurement skills at home—length, width, area, height, volume or capacity, weight, temperature, and time.

☐ 16. Take your child to plays and talk about what makes a good production.

☐ 17. Encourage your child to choose favorite poems and memorize them.

☐ 18. Have your child read a biography of someone he or she admires and discuss it with you.

☐ 19. Help your child read charts, maps, and graphs in newspapers and magazines.

☐ 20. Help your child use study skills, such as skimming, outlining, and note taking, or demonstrate how you use them (for example, how you skim the newspaper).

☐ 21. Help your child use his or her understanding of geometry when looking at art and architecture.

☐ 22. Play number games and do math puzzles with your child.

☐ 23. Teach your child to be courteous—taking turns, waiting in line, saying "please" and "thank you."

Remember: The schools cannot do it all alone.

Sample Curriculum Objectives

The curriculum objectives for Grade 2 Art that follow are a sample of our translation of state standards into more specific grade-by-grade objectives that can be used more easily by teachers. Objectives like these serve as the basis for our work with committees of teachers in school districts that are trying to create their own local district objectives. This sample is drawn from Connecticut and has been used by school districts there to create their own local district objectives.

While your local district objectives will not look exactly like these, they should be similar to these in terms of comprehensiveness, rigor, specificity, clarity of language, and quantity.

Go examine your own district objectives, if you have not already done so. Look at your objectives in all of the subjects and all of the grades—not just at Grade 2 Art, of course. It may be the most important thing you can do as a board member.

Grade 2 Art Objectives

Elements and Principles

☐ **1.** Discusses the relative *size* (proportion) of objects in a picture (*2a)

☐ **2.** Explains what produces a *shadow* in a picture (*2a)

☐ **3.** Identifies shadows in a picture and the *shades* of color seen in the shadows (*2a)

☐ **4.** Recognizes that *space* is a characteristic of artworks and identifies both *positive space* and *negative space* in pictures (*2a)

☐ **5.** Translates two-dimensional shapes into three-dimensional forms (e.g., ovals to eggs, squares to boxes) (*2a)

☐ **6.** Identifies *contrast* in artworks (*2a)

☐ **7.** Identifies and discusses more details in artworks, using appropriate art vocabulary (e.g., shape, color, texture, form) (*2b)

☐ **8.** Recognizes that shades of a color can be produced by mixing with black or by mixing with the complementary color (*2a)

☐ **9.** Mixes colors to produce a range of earth tones (*2a)

☐ **10.** Recognizes that bright colors are used in the foreground and muted colors in the background to add depth to a painting (*2b)

☐ **11.** Identifies a *still life* and discusses why the objects in a still life are a good subject for art (*1a, 3a)

☐ **12.** Identifies a *mural* and discusses some good subjects for murals (*1a, 3a)

☐ **13.** Recognizes that the sky meets the ground in a painting (*2b)

☐ **14.** Identifies *found objects* that could be used in the creation of artworks (*1a)

☐ **15.** Uses vocabulary associated with ceramics: *score, slip, kiln,* and *fire* (*1a)

☐ **16.** Discusses the composition of and balance in artworks (e.g., in sculptures, collages) (*2b)

☐ **17.** Identifies the processes of *decoupage* and *glazing* (*1a)

☐ **18.** Differentiates between materials that are *transparent* and *opaque* (*2a)

Media and Art Production

☐ **1.** Uses pencils, markers, crayons, chalk, charcoal, and brush and ink effectively when drawing (*1d)

☐ **2.** Makes and discusses drawings that tell stories from his or her imagination (*2c, 3a, 3b)

☐ **3.** Draws people and objects from direct observation (*1c)

☐ **4.** Draws portraits and self-portraits with appropriate colors, appropriately placed parts on the face and head (e.g., eyes, ears, nose, mouth), and detail in the facial features (e.g., eyelashes, teeth in a smile) (*2c)

☐ **5.** Draws human bodies with the parts in proportion (e.g., how long the arms are compared to the rest of the body) (*2c)

☐ **6.** Draws figures that are making gestures (*1c)

☐ **7.** Draws from direct observation, using contour line (a line around the outside of the object) (*1c, 2c, 3b)

☐ **8.** Draws a landscape with trees and flowers (*1c, 3b)

☐ **9.** Does washes with watercolors (*1c)

☐ **10.** Paints in the style of the Impressionists (e.g., use of color, type of brush strokes) (*1c, 2c, 3b, 4c)

☐ **11.** Makes a picture using a crayon resist technique (*1c)

☐ **12.** Creates a collage, using mixed media (e.g., tissue paper, painted paper that is then cut up, yarns) (*1c, 3b)

☐ **13.** Creates a *mosaic*, using cut or torn paper (*1c, 3b)

☐ **14.** Creates a mural with his or her classmates (*1c, 3b)

☐ **15.** Uses a variety of techniques when working with clay, including slab construction, score, and slip (*1d)

☐ **16.** Makes a *coil pot* (*1c)

☐ **17.** Creates a clay sculpture of a figure (e.g., a human figure, an animal) (*1c)

☐ **18.** Creates a wire sculpture in the style of Alexander Calder (*1c, 2c, 3b, 4c)

☐ **19.** Creates a bas-relief sculpture (e.g., with paper and corrugated cardboard to hang on the wall), using the principles of composition and balance (*2c)

☐ **20.** Creates a papier-mâché sculpture (*1c)

☐ **21.** Paints any sculpture he or she has created as the final step in the process (*1c)

☐ **22.** Compares and contrasts sculpting with clay, wire, paper, and papier-mâché and discusses their various effects on the viewer (*1a, 1b)

☐ **23.** Uses decoupage to create an artwork (e.g., on a bottle), with glazing (*1c)

☐ **24.** Makes a totem pole (e.g., from paper towel tubes) in the style of a Native American culture (*1c, 3b, 4c)

☐ **25.** Makes a life-like or animal-like three-dimensional mask in the style of another culture, including adding more texture (e.g., adding feathers) (*1c, 4c)

☐ **26.** Makes acrylic or clay pins (*1c)

☐ **27.** Assists willingly in the clean-up after art activities (*1d)

Art Objectives — Grade 2

History and Cultures

☐ **1.** Observes and discusses the work of Italian artist Leonardo da Vinci (1452-1519) in studying and representing the human figure (*4b, 5b)

☐ **2.** Discusses *Impressionism*, including the Impressionists' use of color, their experimental brush strokes, and what they were trying to portray with their techniques (*3a, 4a, 4b, 5b, 6e)

☐ **3.** Observes and discusses the artworks of French Impressionist Edgar Degas (1834-1917), including his portrayal of the figures of ballerinas in drawings, paintings, and sculptures; French Impressionist Pierre Auguste Renoir (1841-1919), including his interest in portraying people rather than landscapes; and American-born Impressionist Mary Cassatt (1844-1926), including her portraits of mothers and children (*3a, 4b, 5b)

☐ **4.** Observes and discusses the artworks of Dutch Postimpressionist Vincent Van Gogh (1853-1890), including his use of color and brush stroke techniques (*4b, 5b)

☐ **5.** Observes and discusses the use of line and color in the works of French artist Henri Matisse (1869-1954) (*4b, 5b)

☐ **6.** Observes and discusses the American scenes and *folk art* of Anna Mary Robertson (Grandma) Moses (1860-1961), Thomas Hart Benton (1889-1975), and Jacob Lawrence (1917-2000) and discusses the purposes they had for creating their art (*3a, 4b, 5a, 6e)

☐ **7.** Observes and discusses *The Saturday Evening Post* covers of American illustrator Norman Rockwell (1894-1978) and his portrayal of everyday situations in American life (*3a, 4b, 5a)

☐ **8.** Discusses the portrayal of common individuals as the content for the artworks of many American artists (e.g., Rockwell, Moses, Benton) (*3a, 5a)

☐ **9.** Observes and discusses the representation of form in Cubist artworks by American painter Stuart Davis (1894-1964) (*4b, 5b)

☐ **10.** Observes and discusses the circus sculptures of American sculptor Alexander Calder (1898-1976), including their characteristic art elements (e.g., form, color) (*4b)

☐ **11.** Observes and discusses the murals of Mexican painter Diego Rivera (1886-1957) and his portrayal of Mexican history and life and compares them to the murals of South Africa (*3a, 4b, 5a)

☐ **12.** Observes and discusses ancient pottery (e.g., examples from Mexico, Greece, Egypt, Pompeii) and recognizes that the earliest civilizations used coil pots to obtain their water (*4a, 4b, 5a, 6e)

☐ **13.** Observes and discusses the mosaics of other cultures, including those of early civilizations (e.g., examples from Pompeii) (*4a, 4b, 6e)

☐ **14.** Observes and discusses the artwork of Native American cultures (including totem poles, pottery, and masks) and discusses the role of art in those cultures (*4a, 4b, 5a, 6e)

☐ **15.** Observes and discusses the masks and figures of the Senufo, Baule, and Dan cultures of Côte d'Ivoire and recognizes their original purposes (*4a, 4b, 5a, 6e)

☐ **16.** Recognizes the role of art museums in modern culture and names at least one art museum (*6d)

Connections

☐ **1.** Describes the styles of art and their characteristic elements found in other countries being studied in social studies (*4a, 4b, 5b)

☐ **2.** Creates artwork to accompany a poem that can be related to an art element or medium (e.g., the use of shadow in Robert Louis Stevenson's "My Shadow," the use of the landscape in William Wordsworth's "Daffodils") (*6b)

☐ **3.** Discusses how the visual arts enhance the production of plays through the creation of sets (*6a)

☐ **4.** Discusses Degas' interest in the ballet and his portrayal of ballerinas at work (*3a, 6a)

☐ **5.** Reads a children's biography of an artist and discusses how his or her life influenced the art he or she created (e.g., Rivera, Degas) (*6b, 6e)

☐ **6.** Relates the description of materials as transparent and opaque to the study of light in science (*6b)

☐ **7.** Designs a stamp or poster to commemorate an event in history or to publicize a community project (*6b, 6d)

☐ **8.** Participates in a group to create a multidisciplinary multimedia project (e.g., art and music, art and poetry) that portrays everyday life in America now or in the past (*4c, 6c)

☐ **9.** Observes and discusses ways in which art is a part of his or her community environment (*6d)

Evaluation

☐ **1.** Explains why he or she likes or dislikes given artworks or given styles of art, by referring to specific art elements (e.g., *I liked that Impressionist painting because the colors were bright and the brush strokes were interesting. I did not like that sculpture of a figure because the size of the body parts looked wrong.*) (*5d)

☐ **2.** Compares and contrasts the figures of people in the artworks of Degas, Renoir, Cassatt, Rivera, Rockwell, and Moses; tells which he or she prefers; and discusses why people might prefer another (*1b, 2b, 5c, 5d)

☐ **3.** Compares and contrasts the sculpture of Degas and Calder, tells which he or she prefers, and discusses why people might prefer the other (*1b, 2b, 5c, 5d)

☐ **4.** Recognizes that his or her likes and dislikes in art might be different from those of his or her art teacher (*5c)

☐ **5.** Discusses why various artists chose to create the works they did (e.g., Degas, Rivera, Rockwell) (*5a)

☐ **6.** Describes how the art elements (e.g., space, form) are used in his or her own artworks and discusses their strengths and weaknesses (*5b, 5e)

☐ **7.** Discusses ways to improve his or her technique in drawing, painting, and/or sculpting (*6e)

Appreciation

☐ **1.** Feels comfortable drawing, painting, and/or sculpting (*1c)

☐ **2.** Wants to improve his or her drawing, painting, and/or sculpting (*5e)

☐   *3.* Enjoys making a variety of crafts (e.g., jewelry, weaving) (*1c)

☐   *4.* Admires the work of one or more famous artists (e.g., Rivera, Rockwell, Cassatt, Van Gogh) (*5d)

☐   *5.* Respects the artistic tastes and preferences of classmates (*5c)

☐   *6.* Enjoys looking at art of a variety of styles and from a variety of cultures (*4b, 5d)

☐   *7.* Believes that going to an art museum is an enjoyable way to spend leisure time (*6d)

☐   *8.* Appreciates how artworks can enhance the community (e.g., sculpture in a park, friezes on a building) (*6d)

*Connecticut Arts Curriculum Framework—Content and Performance Standards in Visual Arts
Copyright © 2003 Connecticut School Steps™

Author Biographical Information

Henry M. Brickell began working with school boards when he developed the Davies–Brickell System of School Board Policy Making and Administration with Dan Davies over 40 years ago. It is the prototype for all of the numbered and lettered systems for creating school board policy manuals that are used today in thousands of school districts nationwide.

Having been a high school teacher, an assistant superintendent, a college professor, and a college associate dean, he now serves as the president of Policy Studies in Education (PSE), a not-for-profit educational research, development, and evaluation organization based in Great Neck, New York. PSE undertakes projects for school districts, state education departments, colleges, foundations, and professional associations across the U.S., most often in the areas of curriculum and program development, evaluation, policy making, and survey research.

He has addressed conferences of teachers, administrators, school board members, legislators, and citizens in almost every state for over four decades. He was named one of the first Distinguished Professors of the National Academy for School Executives, operated by AASA for the professional development of administrators. He wrote a landmark book on educational innovation, *Organizing New York State for Educational Change*, and has been a contributing author to numerous other books on research and evaluation. He served as the American Educational Research Association's representative to the Joint Committee on Standards for Educational Evaluation, which published the benchmarks for the sound evaluation of educational programs that are now standard in the profession.

He holds degrees from The Ohio State University, the University of Chicago, and Columbia University.

Regina H. Paul has directed projects at PSE for over 20 years. She specializes in working with teachers and administrators in school districts to raise standards, improve curricula, and develop assessments to judge the results. She has worked with more than 100 school districts of all types from California to Connecticut and from Minnesota to Texas. She is the editor-in-chief of *School Steps*—sets of K–12 curriculum objectives, which further detail state curriculum standards in a number of states so that teachers can meet them more easily. She is also the editor-in-chief of the *Ohio Parallel/Preliminary Proficiency Tests* and the *Michigan Diagnostic Series*—sets of test questions designed to help students meet state proficiency standards.

She has trained school board members for NSBA and co-authored a book with Dr. Brickell, *Time for Curriculum*, published by NSBA to help board members understand their role in curriculum. She has also conducted projects for state education departments; for professional associations, such as the American Council on the Teaching of Foreign Languages and the National Association for the Education of Young Children; and for national organizations, such as the National Committee on Arts for the Handicapped.

She holds degrees from Cornell University and Columbia University.

CPSIA information can be obtained at www.ICGtesting.com
Printed in the USA
LVOW021949280911

248206LV00001B/92/P

9 781578 862092